P9-EKI-731

plated

plated

Weeknight Dinners,
Weekend Feasts, and
Everything in Between

Elana Karp and
Suzanne Dumaine

Photographs by Robert Bredvad

Clarkson Potter/Publishers
New York

Published in the United States by Clarkson Potter/
Publishers, an imprint of the Crown Publishing Group, a
division of Penguin Random House LLC, New York.
www.crownpublishing.com
www.clarksonpotter.com

CLARKSON POTTER is a trademark and POTTER with
colophon is a registered trademark of Penguin Random
House LLC.

Library of Congress Cataloging-in-Publication Data is
available upon request.

ISBN 978-1-101-90393-3
eBook ISBN 978-1-101-90394-0

Printed in Hong Kong

Book design by Debbie Glasserman and Yeon Kim
Cover design by Yeon Kim
Cover photography by Robert Bredvad

10 9 8 7 6 5 4 3 2 1

First Edition

to the platers out there—
we love you all! This book is for you, and
anyone who just really loves dinner.
And lunch. And breakfast.

contents

introduction

ABOUT PLATED
(IT'S NOT JUST THE TITLE OF THIS BOOK)

At Plated, we're all about the power of cooking at home. Dinnertime is meant for slowing down at the end of your day, connecting to real food and real ingredients, and reconnecting with the people you're sharing them with—but sometimes all that is easier said than done.

In 2012, Nick Taranto and Josh Hix, old friends from business school, were both working long hours in finance and struggling to make home-cooking a reality. Instead of spending time at the market and then in the kitchen (applying their admittedly scant culinary skills), they opted for the ease of takeout. But they were tired of eating that way—impersonally, sometimes wastefully, and usually unhealthfully. That's how the food-delivery company Plated was born—with the idea of getting fresh, preportioned ingredients and chef-designed recipes in front of people at home. The goal was to enable anyone to create a meal he or she could be proud of without the hassle and confusion of weekly meal planning.

What began with two guys hunting down salmon fillets and fresh basil at the local grocery store, then hand-packing boxes to send to friends, has since grown into a sizable company that delivers a new way of cooking to customers at home, all across the country. Over the past few years, amid the growing pains of a quickly scaling business, Plated has never strayed from its core mission of helping people cook how they want, and helping them share it with the people they love around their table.

Every box we send out is carefully hand-packed with local, sustainably sourced ingredients at one of our regional facilities, ensuring that everything arrives fresh. Each meal comes with a step-by-step, easy-to-follow recipe card, so home cooks can relax and actually enjoy cooking.

AND ABOUT US

Now that you know about Plated, we thought you might like to get to know your guides a bit better. We're members of the culinary team at Plated. That means it's our responsibility to dream up recipes, put them through rigorous testing, and scour the country for ingredients that will continue to inspire home cooks week after week. With our combined classical training and time working in the food industry, we're proud to have built a Plated culinary program that has developed thousands of different recipes.

Elana stumbled upon Plated back when it was still in the "two guys packing food" stage. At the time, she was working with school-based food education programs. She has grown the culinary program from her own in-home "test kitchen" (her apartment still smells like bacon) to the uniquely designed professional research and development Plated Test Kitchen we work in today.

Suzanne found Plated soon after that, and was an early recipe contributor while working at Food Network. She eventually joined Plated full time, helping to build a culinary team to support what was beginning to look a lot like a real business. Obviously, it turned into one!

But more important than any of our qualifications is the fact that, well, we love food. In a deep, real way that left us no choice but to make it the center of our day, every day—and we're lucky that means it's our job! We discuss our lunch options before we eat breakfast; spend hours contemplating the best melty cheeses; posit hundreds of recipe ideas a week (some of which we wake up thinking about); and light up in the presence of a new restaurant, dish, or food destination. And we care just as much about *sharing* food. For us, the best part of cooking is watching people enjoy what we've made for them. What's the point of patiently creating two-day ramen if not to hear someone try to tell you how good it is while slurping a mouthful of noodles?

WHY WE WROTE THIS BOOK

Our philosophy is that food should be fun. It's about embracing the experience in its entirety—from planning, to prepping, to cooking, and, of course, the satisfaction of actually eating. So how could we encourage other cooks to feel this way, too?

When we sat down to brainstorm our direction for this book, chicken became our inspiration. Specifically, the One-Pan Roasted Rosemary Chicken with Seasonal Vegetables (page 46). Seared, then roasted over a bed of vegetables with a rosemary, garlic, and white wine sauce, this dish utilizes a classic technique, a few simple but reliably delicious flavors, and only one pan. It's a nourishing dish that our customers go crazy over, relishing that "ta-da" moment when it comes sizzling out of the oven with crisp, golden skin. There's just something about setting down a roast chicken on the dinner table that evokes pride—it's the Platonic dinner ideal. Giving customers the tools to feel this way about something they cooked and the type of food they're eating is our motivation every day at Plated, and it serves as the founding principle for this book.

We felt the clearest way to help you feel comfortable and confident in the kitchen is by providing you with core techniques and allowing you to customize from there. As babies of the '80s, our approach can best be described as "choose your own adventure" cooking.

It can be a challenge to keep our favorite recipes interesting day in and day out; the most natural solution is to cook by season. So in our Weeknight Dinners chapter, we aim to inspire you to incorporate seasonality into meal planning by arming you with four variations of seasonal swap-ins for each main dish. Each recipe can be changed up depending on peak produce when you're cooking it, making every single one of them relevant and exciting twelve months of the year.

From there, the book concept took on a life of its own. In Great for Leftovers, we give you solid recipes and show you how to reinvent the leftovers into entirely new meals by adding a few ingredients; we show you how to plan efficiently in Make Ahead with dishes that stand up well to saving; we take you on a kitchen adventure in Weekend Feasts, sharing meals that take a little extra TLC and will taste a little extra delicious for it; and we strategically walk you through the process of cooking a whole menu for any number of occasions in For a Crowd. And On the Side and At the End remind us that sometimes the smaller elements are the ones that steal the show. No matter how much time you have to cook, there is something in this book for you.

We know that time is often the biggest obstacle to cooking at home—grocery shopping, preparing multiple dishes, managing your hunger—all of this requires careful planning. With that in mind, we've organized each recipe step to save you time. Instead of listing preparations next to ingredients in the ingredient list, we instruct you to get everything ready—or *mise en place* in French—as you move through the recipe, to make it more time-efficient. That way, the ingredient list is more of a shopping list, and you know what to prep when so you're not breaking a sweat by the time you first turn on the stove. Cooking should be fun, but it doesn't always have to take all day. We've gone ahead and organized the whole book around how much time you want to spend in the kitchen on any day.

BEFORE YOU HEAD ON YOUR MERRY WAY . . .

We poured our culinary hearts and souls into putting together a cookbook that's at once unique and practical—something we hope becomes an oft-used, tomato sauce–splattered go-to in your kitchen. This book is for you. It's for any cook who wants to know his or her way around the kitchen, and to master what comes out of it.

We couldn't be more excited to share our recipes with you, and we sincerely hope our crazy enthusiasm comes through. Writing this book wasn't always easy, but it was always fun. (And it usually was done over food.) We hope you enjoy using our cookbook at least as much as we enjoyed writing, cooking, and taste-testing it for you.

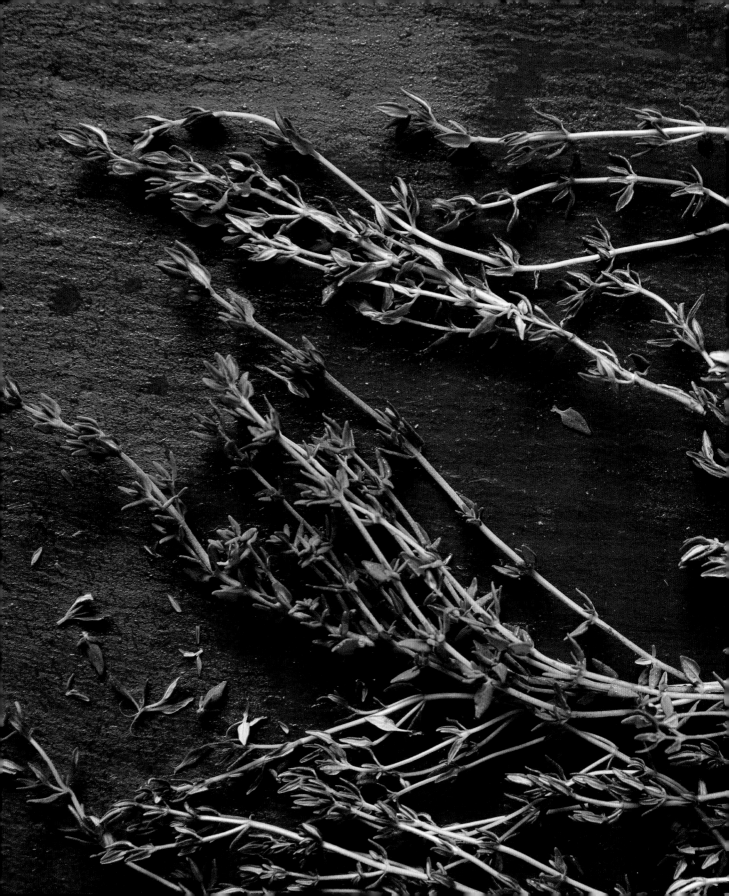

kitchen basics

Before you get cooking, we've put together some handy information that will help you. What follows is a list of kitchen and pantry must-haves and some tips and how-tos to get you on your way. We know you want to dive right in, but if you take a few minutes to read through what's here, you'll save yourself a lot of time (and headaches!) later.

EQUIP YOURSELF

BARE ESSENTIALS

When you're first outfitting your kitchen, these are the basic tools every aspiring chef should have. Most dishes can be made using nothing more than these (with a little MacGyver-ing in some cases).

- Wooden spoon
- 8-inch chef's knife
- Tongs
- Microplane
- Rubber spatula
- Metal spatula
- Chef's knife
- Paring knife
- Colander
- Measuring cups and spoons
- Two rimmed baking sheets
- Large pot
- Medium nonstick pan
- Large ovenproof sauté pan
- Meat thermometer

THE NEXT STEP

You're starting to become a little more experimental in the kitchen, and beginning to use it more! These are some additions to your growing collection that will help make life a little bit easier.

- Cast iron skillet
- Blender or food processor
- Large baking dish
- Fish spatula
- Braising pan with lid
- Small saucepan
- Slotted spoon
- Fine-mesh sieve

GOING ALL OUT

When friends come to your house, they call you "Chef." Sounds pretty sweet, no? You might not have any more room in your kitchen, but you'll want these badass kitchen tools anyway—and we don't blame you.

- Immersion blender
- Grill pan
- Roasting pan
- Stand mixer or hand mixer
- Mandoline slicer
- Spider

STOCKING YOUR PANTRY

These are some basic shelf-stable items you should always have on hand. In a pinch, you could probably make a pretty delicious meal from these alone. They're the foundations you'll rely on for most of the dishes you'll be cooking.

- Extra-virgin olive oil
- Kosher salt
- Tellicherry peppercorns (and a proper pepper grinder)
- Canola oil
- Dijon mustard
- Balsamic vinegar
- Apple cider vinegar or Champagne vinegar
- Honey
- Soy sauce
- Sesame oil
- Chicken or vegetable stock
- Canned diced tomatoes
- White rice
- Quinoa
- Polenta
- Bread crumbs or panko bread crumbs
- All-purpose flour
- Granulated sugar
- Dry pasta
- Canned chickpeas

OUR KITCHEN COMMANDMENTS

STARCHY PASTA COOKING WATER IS LIQUID GOLD
Don't throw it down the sink! When you're making pasta, transfer it directly to the sauce after boiling, along with a few tablespoons of the pasta cooking water. The starch left in the water will create a silky, emulsified sauce seemingly out of thin air, and help it cling to the noodles.

LET IT BE
When you're cooking something that you'd like to get crispy on the outside, resist the temptation to move it around in the pan and check on it. Letting it be will allow for maximum contact with the heat of the pan, giving you the best results. On the other hand, when you're sautéing something you'd like to cook gently without giving it much color (like garlic or onion), stirring more frequently will prevent browning.

SEASON LIKE YOU MEAN IT

When it comes to differentiating good food from great food, a lot comes down to perfect seasoning. Salt and pepper are your food's best friends—season with more of both than you think you should. For salt, scoop up a large pinch using your thumb and first two fingers, and sprinkle it from high above to distribute it as evenly as possible over the food.

THE STOCK MARKET

Stock is meant to be used as the base of the dish, not the defining element. Always buy low-sodium or unsalted stock; salted stock can quickly overpower a dish, and will become exponentially saltier if it's reducing in a soup or stew. Some of our favorite brands are Kitchen Basics and Pacific. If your local butcher happens to sell some homemade stock, well, lucky you. If you make your own, bravo!

SEAR-IOUSLY, DRY YOUR FOOD

Cooking wet food leads to steaming, and therefore to mushy proteins. Take the extra step to (gently) pat your proteins as dry as possible before seasoning and cooking them in fats like oil or butter; you'll get a picture-perfect seared crust. Besides, adding wet proteins can create a splatter that won't feel so good when it hits your hand.

SIZE MATTERS

For consistent cooking times and doneness, cut all your *mise en place* the same size (or as close to it as possible).

GIVE YOUR VEGETABLES SOME (PERSONAL) SPACE

To achieve the perfect golden roasted vegetable, space your vegetables out on the baking sheet. If they're too bunched up, they'll steam from overcrowding. They'll thank you for the room to breathe with their deliciousness.

PATIENCE IS A VIRTUE

We know you're excited to eat, but allow meats to rest for about 10 minutes after cooking and before cutting in. Doing so allows the juices in the meat to redistribute so that when you do make that first slice, they stay in your food, rather than running out all over your cutting board or plate. Keep in mind that your meat will continue cooking while it rests, so if you fear you've undercooked something slightly, chances are it will end up perfect.

SAVE THYME ON HERBS

When you're removing the leaves from rosemary, thyme, tarragon, or oregano, you can save yourself a good 30 minutes with this trick: Hold the stem upright, pinch at the top, and slide your fingers down to strip off the leaves in one fell swoop. For leafier herbs, such as parsley, cilantro, mint, sage, and basil, just pick the whole leaves off. In either case, don't make yourself crazy—a little stem never hurt anyone!

KEEP YOUR HERBS FRESH TO DEATH

The most delicate herbs are softer, leafier varieties like mint and basil. Your best bet for making these last is to stand them up in the fridge in a glass of water that reaches just to where the leaves begin. Alternatively, wrap the stems in a damp paper towel, then wrap the bunch in a loose or perforated plastic bag. Woodier herbs like rosemary and thyme will keep wrapped up in a loose or perforated plastic bag, or in a plastic container in the fridge's crisper drawer if you've got one.

KNOW WHEN THE PAN IS HOT

When you're cooking with oil, the clearest indicator of heat is when ripples begin to appear on the surface of the oil (naturally—not because you stirred it or poked it) and it looks shimmery. At this point it's ideal to add your food; unless specifically directed, don't wait for the oil to start smoking. For cooking with butter, the ideal point is when it begins to foam, but before it begins to turn brown. When you're cooking with a dry pan or grill pan, periodically hover your hand a few inches above it. If you can feel the heat radiating off the pan, it's hot enough. If it merely feels warm, wait another minute and test it again. In all the above instances, sizzling is the sweet sound you should listen for when you add your food to the pan. If you don't hear it, quickly remove your food and allow the pan to continue heating for a few minutes longer.

KNIFE SKILLS

If you're new to cooking, the first thing to master is basic knife skills. You'll be much more efficient (and less likely to cut yourself—or someone else). We've broken down the essentials for how to . . .

CHOOSE YOUR WEAPON

There is a seemingly endless array of fancy, shiny knives in any culinary store, but there are only two you really need: an 8-inch chef's knife and a small paring knife. Expensive Japanese knives look cool, but what's most important is that the knife feels good in your hand. Everyone has personal preferences, so don't worry about the brand. Just find something you feel comfortable using.

HOLD THE KNIFE

Holding a knife correctly will make a huge difference in how safely and quickly you can prep your food. Pinch the bottom of the blade using your thumb and forefinger, and then wrap your other three fingers around the handle. While it might feel weird at first, just keep at it—this grip will give you the best control.

SLICE AND DICE

Holding the knife with one hand, form your other hand into a claw so that your knuckles are exposed, but your fingertips are curled underneath. Hold the ingredient in place with this grip; it will protect your fingertips while keeping everything sturdy as you cut.

For smooth slicing, keep your knife tip on the board and use a rocking motion with the blade to make the cut. Think of it as a back-and-forth rocking motion, rather than a straight up-and-down one (which also won't do your blade any favors).

KEEP THE BLADE SHARP

Keeping your knife sharp is absolutely the most important part of using it well. A dull knife will make every cut about ten times more labor-intensive and frustrating, and is also harder to control (read: fingers in danger). Check for sharpness by holding up a piece of standard printer paper and running the knife into the top. If it slices easily, super! If it doesn't, time to sharpen. If you don't have a knife sharpener, just bring your knives into any store that also sells knives, and they'll likely do it for you.

NOT MESS UP YOUR KNIFE

Keep it far, far away from the dishwasher at all times, under any and all circumstances. Wash gently by hand, scraping away any bits of food, and dry immediately.

SLICE MEAT LIKE A BUTCHER

OK, maybe not quite like a butcher, but close. Slicing meat against the grain is crucial to getting a tender bite. Don't be afraid to actually get close to the meat to ascertain which direction the grains, or grooves, run (hint: it's usually the long way). Be sure to cut perpendicular against that direction, or your perfectly cooked meat could end up tough.

flavoring

Sometimes a sauce, spice rub, marinade, or dressing is all you need to take a dish from good to great. The recipes in this chapter are meant to be building blocks. Sometimes cooking is a little like Jenga, after all. These will crop up throughout the rest of the book, but you may also want to call upon them when you're doing improv in the kitchen. Toss soba noodles with homemade peanut sauce to quickly re-create a perfect version of takeout, or spice up store-bought bread with homemade ricotta. The mix-and-match possibilities are endless (and we're aiming to try them all). Get ready to spice up your life!

SPICE RUBS

When cooking meat or fish over high, direct heat, a rub is perfect for creating a flavorful crust on your food. You can let your protein sit overnight with a rub to allow the flavor to really soak in—but be sure to give it a minimum of 30 minutes to work its magic. When it's time to cook, shake off any excess, then sear, grill, sauté, or roast as desired.

Here are some of our favorites. These recipes all make ¼ cup, which is likely a larger batch than you would need for just one recipe. Combine all the spices, use about 1 teaspoon at a time to lightly coat whatever you're cooking, and save the extra in a jar stored at room temperature for up to 1 month.

southern creole rub

2 teaspoons dried oregano
2 teaspoons sweet paprika
1 teaspoon cayenne pepper
1 teaspoon celery salt
1 teaspoon smoked paprika
½ teaspoon garlic powder
½ teaspoon onion powder
½ teaspoon kosher salt
¼ teaspoon freshly ground
 black pepper

We love it on: fish, shrimp, chicken, and corn

brown sugar barbecue rub

2 tablespoons dark brown
 sugar
2 teaspoons chili powder
2 teaspoons mustard powder
1 teaspoon cayenne pepper
1 teaspoon sweet paprika
½ teaspoon kosher salt
¼ teaspoon freshly ground
 black pepper

We love it on: ribs, steak, and chicken

masala rub

- 1 teaspoon ground cardamom
- 1 teaspoon ground coriander
- 1 teaspoon ground cumin
- 1 teaspoon ground fenugreek
- 1 teaspoon ground turmeric
- ¼ teaspoon ground cinnamon
- ¼ teaspoon ground cloves
- ½ teaspoon kosher salt
- ¼ teaspoon freshly ground black pepper

We love it on: chicken, lamb, eggplant, cauliflower, and chickpeas

mexican chili rub

- 1 tablespoon ground cumin
- 2 teaspoons ancho chile powder
- 2 teaspoons chipotle powder
- 2 teaspoons dried oregano
- 2 teaspoons sweet paprika
- ½ teaspoon kosher salt
- ¼ teaspoon freshly ground black pepper

We love it on: chicken, beef, salmon, shrimp, corn, and winter or summer squash

french herb rub

- 1 tablespoon dried thyme
- 2 teaspoons dried oregano
- 2 teaspoons dried rosemary
- 2 teaspoons dried tarragon
- 1 teaspoon ground fennel
- 1 teaspoon dried marjoram
- ½ teaspoon kosher salt
- ¼ teaspoon freshly ground black pepper

We love it on: chicken, fish, beef, lamb, and vegetables

italian herb rub

- 1 tablespoon dried sage
- 2 tablespoons dried oregano
- 2 teaspoons garlic powder
- 2 tablespoons dried basil
- ½ teaspoon kosher salt
- ¼ teaspoon fresh ground black pepper

We love it on: chicken, fish, and steak

MARINADES

Marinades are ideal for making proteins tender and infusing them with flavor. They're also incredibly hands-off—you can throw meat in a large plastic bag, Tupperware, or bowl with your marinade, forget about it, and have something that's guaranteed to be delicious. With thicker cuts, you can marinate for up to 24 hours. When working with more delicate proteins like fish or shrimp, marinate for no longer than 1 to 2 hours, or the acid in your marinade may start cooking before you get a chance to.

These recipes all yield between ½ and 1 cup marinade. Just mix them all together in whatever vessel you plan to add your protein to. Discard it when you're finished, or, to make an easy sauce, add your marinade to the pan with your protein and cook it to reduce.

mediterranean lemon and herb marinade

MAKES ½ CUP

> Leaves from 4 sprigs fresh
>   oregano, finely chopped
> Leaves from 2 sprigs fresh
>   rosemary, finely chopped
> Leaves from 2 sprigs fresh
>   thyme, finely chopped
> 3 cloves garlic, chopped
> 1 lemon, zested and juiced
> ½ teaspoon crushed red pepper
> ¼ cup extra-virgin olive oil

We love it on: meat, chicken, fish, shellfish, and vegetables

indian yogurt marinade

MAKES ABOUT 1 CUP

> 2 cloves garlic, chopped
> Leaves from 3 sprigs fresh
>   cilantro, roughly chopped
> 1-inch knob fresh ginger,
>   chopped
> ¾ cup Greek yogurt
> 1 teaspoon ground coriander
> 1 teaspoon ground cumin
> 2 tablespoons extra-virgin
>   olive oil

Before cooking, wipe off as much of the marinade as possible.

We love it on: meat and chicken

sesame soy ginger marinade

MAKES ½ CUP

2 cloves garlic, chopped
1-inch knob fresh ginger, chopped
2 tablespoons rice vinegar
2 tablespoons soy sauce
1 tablespoon sesame oil
1 teaspoon agave
1 teaspoon gochujang chile paste (optional)

We love it on: meat, chicken, fish, shellfish, and vegetables

dijon, thyme, and worcestershire marinade

MAKES ½ CUP

2 garlic cloves, smashed
Leaves from 4 sprigs fresh thyme
2 tablespoons Dijon mustard
1 teaspoon balsamic vinegar
1 teaspoon soy sauce
½ teaspoon Worcestershire sauce
¼ cup extra-virgin olive oil

We love it on: steak, pork, and chicken

citrus honey marinade

MAKES ⅔ CUP

1 orange, zested and juiced
1 grapefruit, juiced
1 lemon, juiced
¼ cup white wine
1½ teaspoons honey
¼ teaspoon crushed red pepper (optional)

In a small saucepan, combine the orange zest and juice, grapefruit juice, lemon juice, wine, honey, and crushed red pepper (if using). Bring to a boil over medium-high heat and simmer until reduced by half, about 5 minutes. Allow to cool completely before using, 20 to 25 minutes.

We love it on: chicken, white fish, and shellfish

DRESSINGS

Few things are better than the basics. We're adding the dressings we go back to over and over again in the Plated Test Kitchen to your arsenal. Drizzle them over your favorite salad, toss them with noodles, or pour them into a bowl as a dip for anything and everything.

the perfect vinaigrette

MAKES ⅓ CUP

2 tablespoons Champagne
  vinegar
1 teaspoon Dijon mustard
½ teaspoon honey
3 tablespoons extra-virgin
  olive oil
Kosher salt and freshly ground
  black pepper

In a medium bowl, whisk together the vinegar, mustard, and honey. Season with salt and pepper. Quickly whisk in a figure-eight motion while slowly pouring in the olive oil in a steady stream. Continue until the oil is incorporated and the vinaigrette is emulsified. Taste and add more salt and pepper as needed.

CHEFFY NUGGET: We love this vinaigrette, but it's also a great foundation for making up your own variations. Swap in different acids like lemon juice, or balsamic, apple cider, or white wine vinegar. You can even mix and match with different oils, like grapeseed, walnut, or a combination of canola and olive oil. Our ideal ratio of acid to oil is 2:3.

spicy peanut dressing

MAKES 1 CUP

2 limes, juiced
2 teaspoons soy sauce
2 teaspoons dark brown sugar
½ cup smooth peanut butter
1 teaspoon gochujang chile
  paste
4 tablespoons hot water
Kosher salt

In a medium bowl, stir together the lime juice, soy sauce, and brown sugar until the sugar has dissolved. Add the peanut butter and chile paste and mix until fully combined. Slowly whisk in the hot water, 1 tablespoon at a time, until the sauce is pourable. Taste and add salt as needed.

chicken en papillote

WITH ROASTED SEASONAL VEGETABLES

"En papillote" sounds really impressive, but it's a super-simple cooking technique—and one of our favorites. Whatever goes in your parchment packet is pretty much guaranteed to come out delicious. Try it with any kind of fish fillet, shrimp, or vegetables like mushrooms and carrots. But there's no use in showing this dish off to your friends if you can't pronounce what you're serving. Throw this *PAP-ee-yote* their way and watch them be blown away.

1. Preheat the oven to 400°F.

2. Slice the potatoes crosswise into ¼-inch coins. Thinly slice the lemon.

3. Working on a clean, dry surface, fold 2 large pieces of parchment paper in half, then reopen. Divide the potatoes evenly between them, arranging the slices in a single layer on one side of the fold. Pour the white wine over them and drizzle with 1 teaspoon of the olive oil each. Season with salt and pepper. Season the chicken on both sides with herbes de Provence, salt, and pepper and place on top of the potatoes, then layer the lemon slices and thyme sprigs on top, dividing them evenly.

4. Fold over the parchment paper, re-creasing, then fold in the edges, overlapping and tucking in all around, to create a tightly sealed parcel. Place the papillotes on a baking sheet and bake until the parchment is browned and puffed, and the chicken is cooked through and no longer pink, about 30 minutes.

5. Meanwhile, toss the seasonal vegetables with the remaining 1 tablespoon olive oil, salt, and pepper. Arrange in a single layer on a separate baking sheet. Roast until tender, about 20 minutes.

6. Carefully tear open the papillotes, allowing steam to escape. Discard the thyme sprigs and lemon slices, but serve the chicken and potatoes in the parchment paper for presentation with the roasted seasonal vegetables alongside.

SERVES 2

½ pound fingerling potatoes
1 lemon
2 boneless, skinless chicken breasts
¼ cup white wine
1 tablespoon plus 2 teaspoons extra-virgin olive oil
1 teaspoon herbes de Provence
6 sprigs fresh thyme
Seasonal vegetables (see Seasonal Swaps, opposite)
Kosher salt and freshly ground black pepper

CHEFFY NUGGET: For the best seal on your parchment packet, tuck and crease it as tightly as possible all the way around, or use a dab of beaten egg white on the edges to help them stick. If you don't have parchment handy, foil works well, too.

seared sirloin steak

WITH SEASONAL PANZANELLA SALAD

Panzanella is a salad for the non-salad-lovers. Equal parts crusty bread and fresh, roasted vegetables, this Italian side dish gets better the longer it sits. To change it up, you can replace the ciabatta with cornbread, baguette, sourdough, or any old bread that's lying around. You can't go wrong. We love it with steak, but really, it's good with just about anything.

1. Preheat the oven to 400°F.

2. Cut the ciabatta into large dice. Pick the parsley leaves from the stems. Prepare the seasonal vegetables.

3. On a baking sheet, toss the bread cubes with 2 tablespoons of the olive oil and salt and pepper. Arrange in a single layer and toast until light golden but not too crunchy, about 10 minutes.

4. Meanwhile, make garlic paste (see Cheffy Nugget on page 33). Transfer it to a large bowl and stir in the vinegar and capers. Slowly add 1½ tablespoons of the olive oil, whisking continuously until emulsified. Taste the dressing and add salt and pepper as needed.

5. When the croutons are toasted, add them to the bowl with the dressing and toss to coat. Leave the oven on, but increase the temperature to 425°F if roasting the seasonal vegetables.

6. On the baking sheet used for the bread cubes, toss the seasonal vegetables with 1 tablespoon of the olive oil and salt and pepper. Roast until tender, about 15 minutes.

7. Meanwhile, in a large pan, heat the remaining 1 tablespoon olive oil over medium-high heat. Pat the steak dry and season all over with salt and pepper. When the oil is just smoking, add the steak and cook until browned on the outside and medium-rare, about 5 minutes per side. Remove from the pan and allow to rest for 5 to 10 minutes.

8. Add the roasted seasonal vegetables, parsley, and shaved Parmesan to the croutons and gently toss. Taste and add salt and pepper as needed.

9. Cut the steak against the grain into ¼-inch slices. Serve with the panzanella salad alongside.

SERVES 2

½ large ciabatta roll
¼ bunch fresh flat-leaf parsley
Seasonal vegetables (see Seasonal Swaps, opposite)
5½ tablespoons extra-virgin olive oil
1 clove garlic
1 tablespoon red wine vinegar
2 tablespoons capers
¾ pound sirloin or New York strip steak
¼ cup shaved Parmesan cheese
Kosher salt and freshly ground black pepper

WINTER	SPRING	SUMMER	FALL
1 head escarole, sliced	1 bunch watercress, torn	3 cups baby arugula	1 head red-leaf lettuce, torn

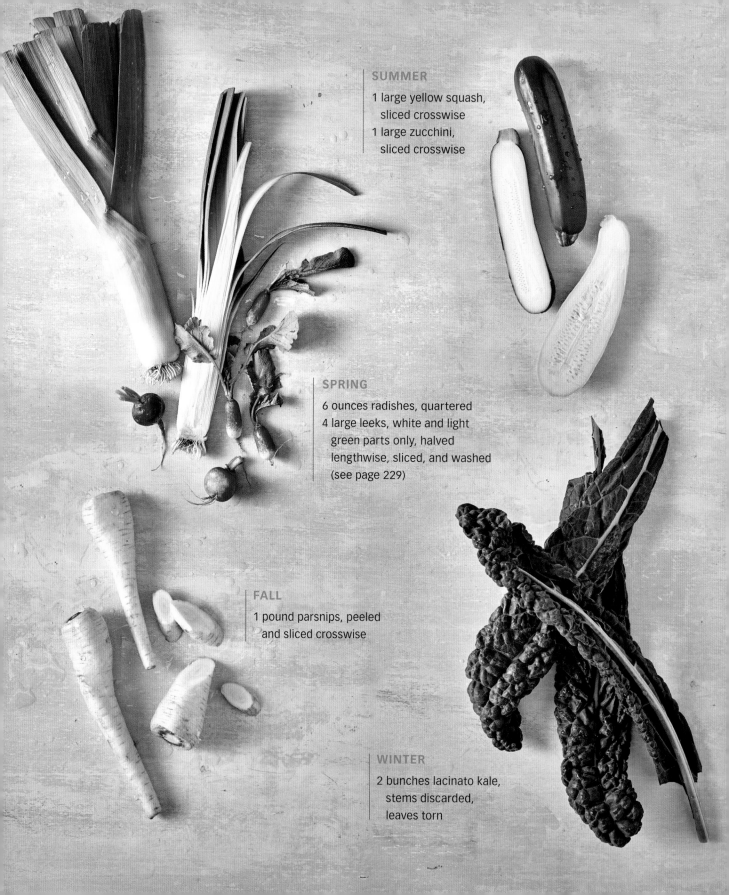

SUMMER

1 large yellow squash,
  sliced crosswise
1 large zucchini,
  sliced crosswise

SPRING

6 ounces radishes, quartered
4 large leeks, white and light
  green parts only, halved
  lengthwise, sliced, and washed
  (see page 229)

FALL

1 pound parsnips, peeled
  and sliced crosswise

WINTER

2 bunches lacinato kale,
  stems discarded,
  leaves torn

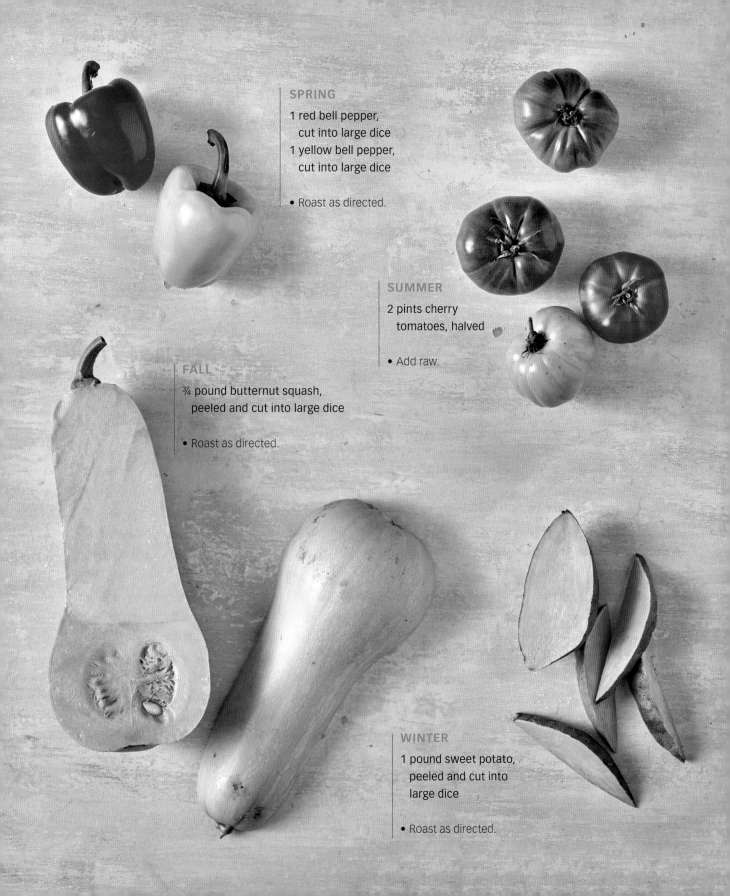

SPRING

1 red bell pepper,
  cut into large dice
1 yellow bell pepper,
  cut into large dice

• Roast as directed.

SUMMER

2 pints cherry
  tomatoes, halved

• Add raw.

FALL

¾ pound butternut squash,
  peeled and cut into large dice

• Roast as directed.

WINTER

1 pound sweet potato,
  peeled and cut into
  large dice

• Roast as directed.

seared tuna

OVER SEASONAL GREENS WITH CARROT-GINGER DRESSING

Doesn't the carrot-ginger dressing at your local Japanese restaurant seem like a magical mystery? If you're anything like us, you can't get enough! Well, we've demystified it, pairing it with lightly seared tuna to re-create a sashimi-style dinner. Much as you want to drink the stuff, we promise this complete meal will be much more satisfying.

1. Peel the ginger, carrot, and shallot and roughly chop. In a blender or food processor, combine the ginger, carrot, shallot, miso, vinegar, half the sesame oil, the grapeseed oil, and 2 tablespoons water. Pulse until smooth. Taste and add salt and pepper as needed.

2. In a medium pan, heat the sesame oil over medium-high heat. Pat the tuna dry and season with salt and pepper. When the oil is just smoking, add the tuna and sear until browned on the outside and rare, about 1 minute per side. Remove to a plate to rest for 5 minutes, then thinly slice.

3. Meanwhile, halve the avocado, discard the pit, and use a spoon to carefully scoop out the whole avocado half. Cut the avocado into ¼-inch slices.

4. Prepare the seasonal greens. Add the avocado, seasonal greens, and edamame to the dressing and toss gently to coat.

5. To serve, fan the sliced tuna over the salad and sprinkle with the sesame seeds.

SERVES 2

Carrot-Ginger Dressing
1½-inch knob fresh ginger
1 medium carrot
1 medium shallot
1 tablespoon white miso
1 tablespoon sesame oil
2 tablespoons grapeseed oil
1 tablespoon rice vinegar
Kosher salt and freshly ground
    pepper

Salad
1 tablespoon sesame oil
2 ahi tuna steaks
1 avocado
Seasonal greens (see Seasonal
    Swaps, below)
1 cup shelled edamame
1 tablespoon white sesame
    seeds
Kosher salt and freshly ground
    black pepper

WINTER	SPRING	SUMMER	FALL
4 cups shredded napa cabbage	6 heads Little Gem lettuce, quartered through the roots	2 heads butter lettuce, torn	1 head escarole, sliced

lamb koftas

WITH PISTACHIOS AND SEASONAL VEGETABLE FARRO

This recipe is a bona fide Plated hit that our book wouldn't be complete without. Pistachios, as well as a host of warm spices like sumac and cumin, are mixed right into the meat to add some crunchy texture. Chewy farro and creamy, lemony yogurt sauce perfectly complement and contrast.

1. Preheat the oven to 425°F if roasting seasonal vegetables (see Seasonal Swaps).

2. Prepare the seasonal vegetables according to the instructions in Seasonal Swaps. If roasting, roast them now.

3. Bring a medium pot of water to a boil over high heat. Add the farro and a generous pinch of salt to the boiling water and cook until tender, 13 to 15 minutes.

4. Meanwhile, finely chop the pistachios. Pick the mint and parsley leaves off the stems. Halve the lemon. Thinly slice the red onion. In a small bowl, mix together the cumin, sumac, thyme, and chili powder.

5. In a medium bowl, combine the pistachios, beef, lamb, and two-thirds of the spice mix. Season with salt and pepper. Mix by hand until fully combined, then divide into 4 equal portions and shape into 3-inch logs to create koftas.

6. In a large pan, heat 1 teaspoon of the olive oil over medium-high heat until shimmering. Add the lamb koftas and cook until browned on the outside and medium-rare, 2 to 3 minutes per side, 8 to 12 minutes total.

7. In a small bowl, stir together the yogurt, juice of ½ lemon, and remaining spice mix. Taste and add salt and pepper as needed. In a separate bowl, toss the mint, parsley, and red onion with a squeeze of lemon juice and 1 teaspoon of the olive oil.

8. Drain the farro. Add the seasonal vegetables and remaining 1 tablespoon olive oil and toss to combine. Taste and add salt and pepper.

9. Serve the koftas over the farro, drizzled with the yogurt sauce, with the herb salad on top as a garnish.

SERVES 2

Seasonal vegetables
  (see Seasonal Swaps,
  opposite)
1 cup pearled farro
1 tablespoon pistachios
½ bunch fresh mint
¼ bunch fresh flat-leaf parsley
1 lemon
½ red onion
1 teaspoon ground cumin
1 teaspoon sumac
1 teaspoon dried thyme
½ teaspoon chili powder
5 ounces ground beef
5 ounces ground lamb
1 tablespoon plus 2 teaspoons
  extra-virgin olive oil
¾ cup Greek yogurt
Kosher salt and freshly ground
  black pepper

CHEFFY NUGGET: Making the koftas all the same size and shape will ensure that they cook evenly.

WINTER

10 ounces mixed red and
golden beets, peeled
and cut into large dice

- Roast at 425°F for 25 to
30 minutes.

SPRING

2 cups shelled fresh fava
beans (see page 229)
3 scallions, thinly sliced

- Add raw.

SUMMER

1½ cups sugar snap peas,
thinly sliced on a diagonal
Leaves from 1 bunch fresh
basil, torn

- Add raw.

FALL

1 delicata squash,
halved lengthwise
and sliced
crosswise

- Roast at 425°F for
15 minutes.

pizza for every season

These are four of our absolute favorite pizzas. The breakfast pizza for Spring was a happy accident in our test kitchen—let's just say it had restorative powers after a long Thursday night. The Summer pizza is a straight riff on rigatoni alla Norma, one of our favorite pasta dishes, while the Fall version pairs sweet, seasonal figs with salty prosciutto. We've saved our heartiest version for Winter—tangy Taleggio with acorn squash and sausage.

1. Preheat the oven to 450°F. Line a baking sheet with parchment paper.

2. Prepare the seasonal pizza toppings according to the instructions in Seasonal Swaps.

3. Meanwhile, sprinkle the flour over a clean, dry surface. Using a rolling pin, roll out the dough as thinly as possible, rotating and flipping it to get the most even rectangular shape, about ⅛ inch thick.

4. Transfer the dough to the prepared baking sheet. Assemble the pizza as directed and bake until the crust is golden, the cheese is melted, and the seasonal ingredients are warmed through, about 15 minutes total.

5. Cut into slices and serve.

SERVES 2

Seasonal pizza toppings
   (see Seasonal Swaps,
   opposite)
1 tablespoon all-purpose flour
1 pound store-bought pizza
   dough
2 tablespoons grated Parmesan
   or pecorino cheese
Kosher salt and freshly ground
   black pepper

FALL

5 fresh black figs or dried figs,
  quartered
1 small red onion, halved and sliced
1 tablespoon extra-virgin olive oil
1 tablespoon balsamic vinegar
2 ounces goat cheese
3 ounces prosciutto
Kosher salt and freshly ground black pepper

- Cook the onion in the olive oil over medium heat,
  seasoning with salt and pepper, until browning,
  about 10 minutes. Add the vinegar and cook until
  sticky, about 2 minutes longer.
- To assemble: Put down a layer of Parmesan, then
  figs, then onion.
- Bake for 10 minutes, then scatter with the goat
  cheese and bake for 5 minutes longer. Top with the
  prosciutto before slicing.

SPRING

1 russet potato, sliced
2 scallions, sliced
1 tablespoon plus 1 teaspoon extra-virgin olive oil
3 ounces goat cheese
2 large eggs
½ cup arugula
Kosher salt and freshly ground black pepper

- Sauté the potato and scallions in 1 tablespoon of
  the olive oil over medium-high heat until softened,
  6 to 8 minutes, then season to taste.
- To assemble: Put down a layer of potatoes and
  scallions and top with the goat cheese.
- When the pizza is halfway baked, carefully place
  the eggs on top, season, and continue baking until
  the whites are set, 7 to 8 minutes. Toss the arugula
  with the remaining 1 teaspoon olive oil and scatter
  over the finished pizza before slicing.

WINTER

1 small acorn squash, halved and
  thinly sliced
1 tablespoon extra-virgin olive oil
6 ounces Italian sausage, casings removed
3 ounces Taleggio cheese, shredded
Kosher salt and freshly ground black pepper

- Toss the squash with the olive oil and salt and
  pepper and roast at 450°F until tender, 15 to
  20 minutes. Meanwhile, sauté the sausage
  over medium heat until browned, breaking
  it up, about 6 minutes.
- To assemble: Put down a layer of
  Taleggio, then squash, then
  sausage. Bake as directed.

SUMMER

1 Italian eggplant, halved lengthwise and sliced
  crosswise
1 tablespoon extra-virgin olive oil
½ cup marinara sauce
3 ounces fresh mozzarella cheese, torn
1 ounce grated or crumbled ricotta salata cheese
Leaves from 1 sprig fresh basil, torn

- Sauté the eggplant in the olive oil over medium-
  high heat until golden and crisping around the
  edges, about 10 minutes, then season to taste.
- To assemble: Put down a layer of marinara, then
  eggplant, then the cheeses. Bake as directed.
- Top with the basil before slicing.

thai red chicken curry

WITH STICKY RICE AND SEASONAL VEGETABLES

All curry pastes are different, and the selection in your grocery store will be endless. Try out a few brands in order to find your favorite, keeping in mind that they vary in heat level and intensity. You also might want to taste a little bit before adding it to your food to see how hot it is. We've both come across sticky rice in our Southeast Asian travels, which lends an authenticity to this dish—plus, it's fun to knead.

1. In a small saucepan, combine the sticky rice, water, and a pinch of salt and bring to a boil over high heat. Once it comes to a boil, stir once, cover, and reduce the heat to low. Simmer for 12 minutes, then remove from the heat and allow to steam, still covered, for about 10 minutes. Uncover, fluff the rice with a fork, then cover and set aside.

2. While the rice cooks, prepare the seasonal vegetables. Mince the garlic and dice the onion. Peel and mince the ginger.

3. In a large sauté pan, heat 1 tablespoon of the canola oil over medium-high heat. Season the chicken on both sides with salt and pepper. When the oil is shimmering, add the chicken and sear until browned on the outside, 2 to 3 minutes per side. Transfer to a plate and set aside.

4. Heat the remaining 1 tablespoon canola oil in the same pan over medium heat. When the oil is shimmering, add the onion, garlic, and ginger. Sauté until the onion is soft and translucent and the garlic and ginger are fragrant, about 5 minutes. Stir in the curry powder and turmeric and cook until fragrant, about 1 minute longer.

5. Add the seasonal vegetables (but reserve the leafy greens, if using, including kale), season with salt, and cook until softened, 5 to 8 minutes longer.

6. Add the curry paste and stir to combine. Cook, stirring, for about 1 minute. Stir in the coconut milk and stock. Increase the heat to high and bring to a boil, then reduce the heat to medium-low and simmer for 7 to 8 minutes to meld the flavors and reduce slightly. Add the reserved seasonal leafy greens, stir to combine, and cook until just beginning to wilt, about 2 minutes.

SERVES 2

- ¾ cup sticky rice
- 1¼ cups water
- Seasonal vegetables (see Seasonal Swaps, opposite)
- 2 cloves garlic
- 1 yellow onion
- 1-inch knob fresh ginger
- 2 tablespoons canola oil
- ¾ pound boneless, skinless chicken thighs
- ½ tablespoon curry powder
- 1 teaspoon ground turmeric
- 2 tablespoons red curry paste
- 1 cup coconut milk
- 1 cup low-sodium chicken stock
- 2 sprigs fresh regular or Thai basil
- Kosher salt and freshly ground black pepper

7. Nestle the chicken into the broth, mostly submerging it. Increase the heat to high and return to a boil, then reduce the heat to medium and braise the chicken until opaque and cooked through, about 6 minutes.

8. Meanwhile, pour the rice out onto a clean dry surface. Using a wooden spoon or spatula, pat it down into an even layer. Fold it over itself, then pat it down into an even layer again. Continue kneading until the grains begin to stick together and the steam is released, 2 to 3 minutes. Mound the rice into 2 balls and place in shallow bowls.

9. Taste the curry and add salt and pepper as needed. Pick the basil leaves from the stems and stir the leaves into the curry. To serve, ladle the chicken and curry over the sticky rice.

CHEFFY NUGGET: Kneading the sticky rice evaporates its moisture, encouraging the grains to stick together, rather than to the pot, the cutting board, or your bowl. Continue the process until you can pick up a small ball of rice and it holds its shape without sticking to your fingers. If you'd rather, you can use white rice and skip the kneading—but we think it's kind of fun.

WINTER	SPRING	SUMMER	FALL
2 cups cauliflower florets	8 ounces new potatoes, cut into medium dice	12 ounces baby or graffiti eggplant, cut into medium dice	½ bunch mustard greens, stems discarded, leaves torn
½ bunch (6 ounces) curly kale, stems discarded, leaves torn	3 cups baby spinach		8 ounces cremini mushrooms, sliced

cheesy baked penne

WITH CREAMY TOMATO SAUCE AND SEASONAL VEGETABLES

This recipe offers a grown-up way to eat baked ziti: three delicious cheeses, vodka sauce, and some vegetables for good measure. Easily doubled or even tripled, this recipe is ideal for potlucks or dinner parties—and you can assemble it ahead of time and bake it just before serving.

1. Preheat the oven to 400°F.

2. Bring a large pot of water to a boil over high heat for the pasta.

3. Prepare the seasonal vegetables. Mince the garlic. Cut half the mozzarella into ¼-inch dice and thinly slice the remainder. Roughly tear the basil leaves. Roughly chop the oregano leaves. Strip the thyme leaves from the stems.

4. Add the penne and a generous pinch of salt to the boiling water. Cook until just a bit too al dente to eat, with a slight bite, about 2 minutes less than the lower range on the package instructions. Drain the pasta.

5. Meanwhile, in a large ovenproof sauté pan, heat the olive oil over medium-high heat until shimmering. Add the seasonal vegetables, oregano, thyme, crushed red pepper, salt, and pepper. Sauté until slightly tender, about 5 minutes. Add the tomato sauce, stir to combine, and bring to a simmer. Taste and add salt and pepper as needed. Remove the pan from the heat.

6. Add the drained penne to the vegetables and stir to combine. Add the ricotta and cubed mozzarella and stir to distribute evenly. Pat down into an even layer, then scatter the sliced mozzarella and grated Parmesan on top.

7. Cover with foil and bake until the sauce is bubbling around the sides, 15 to 20 minutes. Remove from the oven and turn the broiler to high. Uncover the penne and broil until the cheese is golden and bubbling, 3 to 5 minutes.

8. Allow the penne to cool for about 5 minutes, then garnish with the basil and serve.

SERVES 2

Seasonal vegetables
(see Seasonal Swaps,
opposite)
2 cloves garlic
4 ounces fresh mozzarella
cheese
2 sprigs fresh basil
1 sprig fresh oregano
2 sprigs fresh thyme
8 ounces penne pasta
1½ tablespoons extra-virgin
olive oil
¼ teaspoon crushed red
pepper
2 cups Tomato Sauce
alla Vodka (page 35) or
1 14-ounce jar marinara
sauce
⅓ cup ricotta cheese, store-
bought or homemade
(page 40)
1 tablespoon grated
Parmesan or pecorino
cheese
Kosher salt and freshly ground
black pepper

CHEFFY NUGGET: If you don't have an ovenproof pan handy, transfer the penne mixture to a baking dish.

WINTER

½ bunch collard greens, stems and leaves thinly sliced

SPRING

½ bunch asparagus, trimmed and cut into 1-inch pieces

SUMMER

1 large zucchini, quartered lengthwise and sliced crosswise

FALL

8 ounces cremini or wild mushrooms, sliced

great for leftovers

If you're like us and love the day after Thanksgiving even more than you love the day of, you might just be a leftover fiend. This chapter includes simple recipes that are easy to make in large batches, with leftovers at top of mind. We'll show how, by adding only one or two ingredients, you can repurpose these dishes into an entirely new meal. Each initial recipe makes two servings to eat right away, plus enough for two servings of the leftovers recipe as well.

homemade potato gnocchi

WITH BROWN BUTTER AND SAGE

These gnocchi are the real deal. About ten years ago in Italy, Elana learned how to make them from a real Sicilian *nonna*—and now, she's something of a gnocchi whisperer. One of the most important secrets we've learned to achieving pillowy, fluffy gnocchi is that it's easier than it looks. Once you've made a full batch of the stuff, you can set aside half to bake into a totally new recipe; the remaining gnocchi will keep in the fridge for up to 2 days.

1. Pierce the potatoes all over with a fork and microwave until tender, 8 to 12 minutes, turning halfway through. Remove and set aside until cool enough to handle.

2. Bring a large pot of water to a boil over high heat for the gnocchi.

3. Halve the potato lengthwise and carefully scoop out the flesh into a large bowl (discard the skins). Add the egg and flour. Knead by hand until the mixture is fully combined and it reaches a dough-like consistency. If the dough is too wet, knead in more flour, 1 tablespoon at a time. Form the potato mixture into a ball and turn it out onto a dry, flour-dusted surface. Cut the dough into 4 equal portions.

4. Dust a clean, dry surface lightly with flour. Roll one portion of the dough into a rope about ½ inch thick. As you roll, allow your fingers to widen, helping the dough spread out evenly. Then, cut the rope crosswise into ¾-inch pieces. Repeat with the remaining 3 portions of dough.

5. Thinly slice the sage leaves. In a large nonstick pan, heat the butter and sage together over medium-high heat, constantly swirling until the butter is nutty, fragrant, and golden brown, 3 to 4 minutes. Remove from the heat and set aside.

6. Working in batches, add the gnocchi and a generous pinch of salt to the pot of boiling water. Boil until they float to the top, 2 to 3 minutes. Meanwhile, return the pan with the butter to low heat. Carefully scoop out the gnocchi using a slotted spoon or spider, reserving the pasta cooking water. Transfer half the gnocchi to the pan with the butter.

SERVES 2 + 2 LEFTOVERS

1 pound russet potatoes
1 large egg
¼ cup all-purpose flour, plus more for kneading and dusting
5 sprigs fresh sage
8 tablespoons (1 stick) unsalted butter
¼ cup grated Parmesan cheese
Kosher salt and freshly ground black pepper

CHEFFY NUGGET: Imagine giving gnocchi "jazz hands" when you're rolling the dough into a log. Spreading out your fingers will help naturally elongate the dough, rather than forcing it.

Transfer the remaining gnocchi to a medium bowl and set aside to cool. Once cool, drizzle with olive oil and save for leftovers. Refrigerate, covered with plastic wrap, for up to 2 days.

7. Warm the gnocchi in the brown butter until well coated and beginning to brown, about 5 minutes. Add the pasta cooking water, 1 tablespoon at a time, until the sauce clings to the gnocchi. Remove the pan from the heat and stir in half the Parmesan cheese. Taste and add salt and pepper as needed.

8. Serve the gnocchi with the remaining Parmesan sprinkled on top.

LEFTOVERS

baked gnocchi with
tomato sauce and mozzarella

1. Preheat the oven to 425°F.

2. In a medium ovenproof baking dish, combine the leftover gnocchi with enough marinara sauce to cover. Sprinkle the mozzarella evenly on top. Bake until the sauce is bubbling and the cheese is golden, 10 to 12 minutes. Serve hot.

SERVES 2

Leftover gnocchi
1 14-ounce jar marinara sauce
   or Marinara (page 35)
1 cup shredded mozzarella
   cheese

roasted carrot and chickpea salad

OVER QUINOA

When you roast carrots, they take on the perfect slight sweetness—and we love the way spicy harissa complements that flavor. The leftovers from this simple salad can be whipped up into an unrecognizable separate dish: an Indian-inspired soup that reuses crispy chickpeas as a crunchy garnish.

1. Preheat the oven to 425°F.

2. Bring a medium pot of water to a boil over high heat for the quinoa.

3. Peel the carrots and trim the leafy tops, leaving ½ inch of the stems. Halve lengthwise. Drain and rinse the chickpeas. Thinly slice the mint leaves.

4. Add the quinoa and a generous pinch of salt to the boiling water and cook until tender, about 15 minutes. Drain and set aside.

5. While the quinoa cooks, on a baking sheet, toss the chickpeas with ½ tablespoon of the harissa, ⅛ teaspoon of the cumin, 1 tablespoon of the olive oil, salt, and pepper. Arrange in a single layer and roast for about 10 minutes.

6. Meanwhile, in a large bowl, toss the carrots with the remaining ½ tablespoon harissa, ⅛ teaspoon cumin, 1 tablespoon of the olive oil, salt, and pepper. When the chickpeas have roasted for 10 minutes, add the carrots to the baking sheet and roast until the chickpeas are crisp and the carrots are tender, about 15 minutes longer.

> Set aside half the roasted carrot-chickpea mixture and save for leftovers. Let cool, then store, covered, in the fridge for up to 4 days.

7. While the vegetables roast, in a small bowl, whisk together the lemon juice, honey, and remaining 1 tablespoon olive oil. Taste and add salt and pepper as needed.

8. Drizzle the quinoa with the dressing, top with the carrots and chickpeas, and garnish with the feta and mint.

SERVES 2 + 2 LEFTOVERS

- 1 pound carrots, with tops
- 1 15-ounce can chickpeas
- ¼ bunch fresh mint
- ⅔ cup red quinoa
- 1 tablespoon harissa paste
- ¼ teaspoon ground cumin
- 3 tablespoons extra-virgin olive oil
- ½ lemon
- 1 teaspoon honey
- ¼ cup crumbled feta cheese
- Kosher salt and freshly ground black pepper

(recipe continues)

coconut carrot soup
with crispy chickpeas

1. Preheat the oven to 425°F.

2. Peel and mince the ginger. Roughly chop the roasted carrots, discarding any stems.

3. In a medium pot, heat the oil over medium heat until shimmering. Add the ginger and carrots and cook until warmed through, about 3 minutes. Add the coconut milk and vegetable stock and stir to combine. Increase the heat to high and bring to a boil, then reduce the heat to medium and simmer until the liquid is thickened, 15 to 20 minutes.

4. While the soup simmers, place the leftover chickpeas on a baking sheet and warm in the oven to re-crisp, about 10 minutes.

5. Use an immersion blender to blend until smooth. (Or transfer to a blender or food processor and blend, taking care to avoid splattering.) Taste and add salt and pepper as needed. Serve garnished with the crispy chickpeas.

SERVES 2

1½-inch knob fresh ginger
Leftover roasted chickpeas and
  carrots
1 tablespoon canola oil
½ cup coconut milk
3 cups vegetable stock
Kosher salt and freshly ground
  black pepper

pesto-grilled chicken kebabs

WITH RICOTTA PEA SALAD

1. Heat a grill to high or a grill pan over high heat.

2. Cut the chicken into 1-inch cubes. In a large bowl, toss the chicken with ⅓ cup of the pesto to coat. Marinate for at least 15 minutes at room temperature (or cover with plastic wrap and marinate overnight in the fridge).

3. Pick the tarragon leaves off the stems. Mince the shallot. Halve the snap peas on a diagonal. Halve the lemon. Cut the white and light-green parts of the scallions into 1-inch pieces (discard the dark green tops).

4. When the grill or grill pan is hot, add the lemon, cut-side down. Grill, without moving, until charred and juicy, 2 to 3 minutes. Squeeze the juice into a large bowl. Whisk in the honey, tarragon, and shallot. While whisking, slowly stream in 2 tablespoons of the olive oil to emulsify. Taste and add salt and pepper as needed. Set the lemon vinaigrette aside.

5. Thread skewers, alternating chicken with scallion, about 4 pieces of each. Season on both sides with salt and pepper. Brush the grill or grill pan with the remaining 2 tablespoons olive oil. Add the kebabs and grill, brushing with some of the remaining pesto every 1 to 2 minutes, until the chicken is cooked through, 3 to 4 minutes per side.

6. While the kebabs grill, in a medium pot, bring the stock to a boil over medium heat. Add the snap peas and shelled peas and cook until bright green and tender, about 2 minutes. Drain and rinse under cold water. Add to the lemon vinaigrette along with the pea shoots. Toss to coat just before serving. Taste the salad and add salt and pepper as needed.

> Set aside half the chicken kebabs and half the pea salad to save for leftovers. Pull the chicken and scallions off the skewers. Cover and store the chicken and salad separately in the fridge for up to 4 days.

7. To serve, dollop the pea salad with the ricotta and top with the kebabs.

SERVES 2 + 2 LEFTOVERS

- 1½ **pounds boneless, skinless chicken breasts**
- ½ **cup pesto, store-bought or homemade (page 39)**
- 4 **sprigs fresh tarragon**
- 1 **shallot**
- 2 **cups sugar snap peas**
- 1 **lemon**
- 4 **scallions**
- ½ **tablespoon honey**
- 4 **tablespoons extra-virgin olive oil**
- 2 **cups chicken stock or water**
- 2 **cups shelled fresh peas**
- 2 **cups pea shoots**
- ¼ **cup ricotta cheese, store-bought or homemade (page 40)**
- **Kosher salt and freshly ground black pepper**

(recipe continues)

pesto chicken pizza with ricotta and peas

1. Preheat the oven to 450°F. Line a baking sheet with parchment paper.

2. Shred the chicken into bite-size pieces.

3. Sprinkle flour over a clean, dry surface. Roll out the pizza dough as thinly as possible into a rectangle, about ⅛ inch thick, flipping and rotating the dough between each roll. Transfer the dough to the lined baking sheet.

4. Spread the pesto evenly over the pizza, leaving a 1-inch border. Drizzle with the olive oil and lightly season with salt. Dot with the ricotta. Bake the pizza until the crust is crisp, about 15 minutes.

5. Remove from the oven, scatter the shredded chicken and scallions on top, and return to the oven until warmed through, about 3 minutes. Garnish with the pea salad before slicing and serving.

SERVES 2

Leftover pesto-grilled chicken and scallions (off the skewers)

All-purpose flour, for dusting

1 pound store-bought pizza dough

2 tablespoons pesto, store-bought or homemade (page 39)

1 tablespoon extra-virgin olive oil

¼ cup ricotta cheese, store-bought or homemade (page 40)

Leftover pea salad

Kosher salt

herb-marinated steak

WITH TOMATO, ONION, AND HERB SALAD

Skirt steak is an ideal cut for quickly soaking up flavor (and then cooking in even less time), plus it will hold up all week long. Marinated onions and tomatoes soften as they sit and make for especially great leftovers in sandwiches, on their own as a salad, or, in this case, tucked into a gyro.

1. Roughly chop the rosemary, oregano, and thyme leaves. Roughly chop the garlic. Zest 1 lemon and halve both.

2. In a medium bowl, combine the rosemary, oregano, thyme, garlic, lemon zest, juice of 1 lemon, and the crushed red pepper. While whisking, slowly add 2 tablespoons of the olive oil. Add to a large resealable plastic bag along with the steak, shake to coat, and set aside to marinate for at least 30 minutes at room temperature or overnight in the fridge.

3. While the steak marinates, cut the tomatoes into ½-inch wedges (or halve them, if using grape). Halve the onion and slice it as thinly as possible. Pick the parsley and basil leaves from the stems.

4. In a large bowl, whisk together the juice of the remaining lemon and 2 tablespoons olive oil to make the dressing. Taste and add salt and pepper as needed. Set aside.

5. Heat a grill to medium-high or a grill pan over medium-high heat. Remove the steak from the marinade, allowing the excess to drip off. Season generously on both sides with salt and pepper. When the grill or pan is hot, add the steak and cook until browned on the outside and medium-rare, about 3 minutes per side. Remove and set aside to rest for 5 to 10 minutes before thinly slicing against the grain.

6. While the steak rests, add the tomatoes, onion, parsley, basil, and feta to the bowl with the dressing and toss to coat.

> Before serving, set aside half the steak and half the tomato salad and save for leftovers. Store separately in the refrigerator for 1 to 2 days.

7. Serve the steak with the salad alongside.

SERVES 2 + 2 LEFTOVERS

- 1 sprig fresh rosemary
- 2 sprigs fresh oregano
- 1 sprig fresh thyme
- 1 clove garlic
- 2 lemons
- ¼ teaspoon crushed red pepper
- 4 tablespoons extra-virgin olive oil
- 1½ pounds skirt steak
- 5 beefsteak or heirloom tomatoes, or 2 cups grape tomatoes (whatever's in season)
- 1 small red onion
- ¼ bunch fresh flat-leaf parsley
- ¼ bunch fresh basil
- ⅓ cup crumbled feta cheese
- Kosher salt and freshly ground black pepper

(recipe continues)

steak gyros with yogurt sauce

1. Toast the pitas. Season the Greek yogurt with salt and pepper.

2. Top the pita with steak and salad, dollop with the Greek yogurt, and serve.

SERVES 2

2 large pitas
¾ cup Greek yogurt
Leftover steak
Leftover tomato, onion, and
  herb salad
Kosher salt and freshly ground
  black pepper

mustard-roasted salmon

WITH CRISPY CAPERS AND ORZO RISOTTO

This dish combines a few of our most favorite things: mustard, briny capers—roasted here as a crispy garnish—and orzo cooked risotto-style until super creamy. We secretly love when orzo cools and becomes sticky, so we're utilizing that texture as a "glue" in the leftovers recipe, another of our favorite dishes: crispy, herby, salmon cakes.

1. Preheat the oven to 400°F.

2. Roughly chop the dill and parsley leaves. Finely dice the onion.

3. In a medium pot, bring the stock to a simmer over medium-high heat, then cover and reduce the heat to low to keep warm.

4. In a large sauté pan, melt the butter over medium-high heat. When the butter is foamy, add the onion and sauté until soft and translucent, 3 to 4 minutes. Add the orzo and stir to coat. Cook until lightly toasted and fragrant, about 2 minutes. Add the wine and stir to combine. Simmer until the pan is almost dry, about 30 seconds. Add the warm stock to the pan, increase the heat to high, and bring to a boil. As soon as it comes to a boil, reduce the heat to medium and simmer, stirring frequently, until tender and creamy, 8 to 10 minutes.

5. While the orzo risotto cooks, in a small bowl, mix together the mustard and 1 tablespoon of the olive oil. Place the salmon skin-side down on a baking sheet and season the flesh with salt and pepper. Spread the mustard evenly over each fillet. Add the capers and the remaining 1 tablespoon olive oil to the bowl that had the mustard and toss to coat. Scatter the capers around the salmon on the baking sheet. Roast until the salmon flakes easily and is medium-rare, about 8 minutes.

6. Turn the broiler to high, transfer the salmon to the top rack, and broil until the mustard browns in spots, 2 to 3 minutes.

7. When the orzo is tender and creamy, remove the pan from the heat and stir in the grated cheese, dill, and parsley. Taste and add salt and pepper as needed.

SERVES 2 + 2 LEFTOVERS

¼ bunch fresh dill
¼ bunch fresh flat-leaf parsley
1 yellow onion
1⅔ cups chicken or vegetable stock
2 tablespoons unsalted butter
1¼ cups orzo
½ cup white wine
2 tablespoons Dijon mustard
2 tablespoons extra-virgin olive oil
4 6-ounce skin-on Atlantic salmon fillets
¼ cup capers
½ cup grated Parmesan cheese
Kosher salt and freshly ground black pepper

> Before serving, set aside half the orzo and half the salmon and capers to use as leftovers. Cover and refrigerate for up to 3 days.

8. To serve, top the orzo with the salmon and capers.

LEFTOVERS

crispy salmon and orzo cakes

1. Using a fork, flake the salmon into small pieces, discarding the skin. In a large bowl, combine the salmon, capers, and orzo. Add the bread crumbs, mayonnaise, and egg and mix to combine. Form the mixture into 6 equal patties and chill in the fridge for 10 to 15 minutes.

2. In a large nonstick pan, heat the olive oil over medium-high heat until shimmering. Add the patties and cook until crisp on the outside and warmed through, 3 to 4 minutes per side. Transfer to a paper towel–lined plate to drain before serving.

SERVES 2

Leftover mustard-roasted
   salmon and capers
Leftover orzo
¼ cup panko bread crumbs
2 tablespoons mayonnaise
1 large egg
2 tablespoons extra-virgin
   olive oil

CHEFFY NUGGET: Usually, the best test for fish doneness is sliding a small knife into the center to see if it meets any resistance. However, unlike other fish, with salmon the knife *should* meet a little resistance, as it's best served medium-rare.

creamy polenta
WITH MUSHROOM RAGOÛT

Using a mix of fresh and dried mushrooms in sauces and soups is ideal; fresh provide meaty texture and heartiness, while dried bring concentrated flavor, released when they're reconstituted. You could use this ragoût over pasta, but we particularly like the way this dish can became an all-in-one leftover: Mix ragoût into polenta, let it harden, then fry it in olive oil. Enjoy it any time of day.

1. In a small saucepan, bring the water to a boil over high heat. As soon as it comes to a boil, add the dried mushrooms, remove from heat, and soak for about 10 minutes.

2. Meanwhile, strip the thyme leaves from the stems. Cut the fresh mushrooms into ¼-inch slices. Thinly slice the shallots. Roughly chop the parsley leaves.

3. Drain the dried mushrooms, reserving the soaking liquid. Roughly chop and pat dry.

4. Heat a large pan over medium-high heat. When the pan is hot, add the dried and fresh mushrooms in a single layer and immediately season with salt and pepper. Cook without moving until beginning to crisp, 3 to 4 minutes. Add the butter, thyme, and shallots. Reduce the heat to medium and cook, stirring, until the mushrooms are tender and browning and the shallots are softened, about 5 minutes.

5. Add the wine, scraping up any browned bits on the bottom of the pan. Increase the heat to medium-high and simmer until the wine is reduced by half, about 3 minutes. Add the reserved mushroom soaking liquid to the pan and continue to simmer until reduced by half, 3 to 4 minutes longer. Reduce the heat to low and keep warm until ready to serve.

6. Meanwhile, in a medium saucepan, bring the chicken stock, milk, and a large pinch of salt to a boil over high heat. As soon as the liquid is boiling, while whisking, slowly add the polenta. Immediately reduce the heat to as low as possible and whisk slowly and continuously until the polenta is tender and all the liquid has been absorbed (cooking time may vary; check package instructions). Remove the pot from the heat and stir in the cheese. Taste and add salt and pepper as needed.

SERVES 2 + 2 LEFTOVERS

- 1 cup water
- ½ cup dried porcini mushrooms
- 6 sprigs fresh thyme
- 1½ pounds mixed fresh mushrooms (we like cremini, oyster, and shiitake)
- 2 shallots
- ¼ bunch fresh flat-leaf parsley
- 2 tablespoons unsalted butter
- ½ cup white wine
- 3 cups chicken or vegetable stock
- 2 cups whole milk
- 2 cups polenta
- ⅓ cup grated Parmesan or pecorino cheese
- Kosher salt and freshly ground black pepper

(recipe continues)

7. Taste the ragoût and add salt and pepper as needed. Remove the pan from the heat and stir in the parsley.

8. To serve, divide half the polenta evenly between 2 bowls and top with half the ragoût.

> Stir the remaining polenta and ragoût together to save as leftovers. Spread into an even layer in a medium baking dish and store, covered, in the fridge for up to 4 days.

LEFTOVERS

polenta cakes with fried eggs

1. Cut the chilled polenta into 3-inch squares. In a large nonstick pan, heat 1 tablespoon of the olive oil over medium-high heat until shimmering. Add the polenta cakes in a single layer and cook until browned and warmed through, about 3 minutes per side. Remove and set aside.

2. Heat the remaining 1 tablespoon oil in the same pan over medium heat. Crack the eggs into the pan and season with salt and pepper. Fry without moving until the whites are set, 2 to 3 minutes. Slide the fried eggs over the polenta cakes and eat hot.

SERVES 2

> Leftover polenta with
>   mushroom ragoût, chilled
> 2 tablespoons extra-virgin
>   olive oil
> 2 large eggs
> Kosher salt and freshly ground
>   black pepper

CHEFFY NUGGET: Polenta has two possible textures: creamy and delicious or totally solid. Make sure you have everything else ready before beginning to cook the polenta; you'll want to eat it as soon as it comes off the stove.

garlicky shrimp stir-fry

WITH SHIITAKES AND BOK CHOY

Rice is pretty much the perfect leftover—in fact, we love purposely making too much, just so we can repurpose it the next day. The steamed rice in this stir-fry is perfect for mopping up sauce, but once the rice dries out, it's no longer a moisture sponge. In the leftover fried rice dish, it crisps up, becoming the star feature.

1. In a medium pot, combine the rice, water, and a pinch of salt and bring to a boil over high heat. As soon as the water comes to a boil, stir once, cover, and reduce the heat to low. Cook for 12 minutes, covered, then remove from the heat. Keep covered and allow to steam for at least 10 minutes.

2. While the rice cooks, cut the bok choy crosswise into ½-inch slices, keeping the leaves and stalks separate. Mince the garlic. Stem the shiitakes and thinly slice the caps. Peel and mince the ginger. In a small bowl, whisk together the stock, cornstarch, and mirin.

3. In a large pan, heat the sesame oil over medium-high heat until shimmering. Add the bok choy stalks and shiitakes, spreading into a single layer. Season with salt and pepper. Cook without moving until starting to brown on the bottom, 2 to 3 minutes. Stir and cook until softening, 2 to 3 minutes. Add the crushed red pepper, garlic, ginger, and bok choy leaves and stir to combine. Cook until fragrant, about 1 minute. Season the shrimp on both sides with salt and pepper. Add to the vegetables and cook until just pink, 1 to 2 minutes per side.

4. Push all the ingredients to the outer edges of the pan. Pour the stock mixture into the center, and simmer until thickened, about 2 minutes. Stir everything together to combine and coat, then remove the pan from the heat. Taste the stir-fry and add salt and pepper as needed.

5. Uncover the rice and fluff with a fork. Taste and add salt and pepper as needed.

> Before serving, set aside half the rice and half the stir-fry to use as leftovers. Cover and refrigerate for up to 3 days.

6. To serve, top the rice with the stir-fry.

SERVES 2 + 2 LEFTOVERS

- 1½ cups jasmine or basmati rice
- 2½ cups water
- 4 baby bok choy
- 4 cloves garlic
- 1 pound shiitake mushrooms
- 1-inch knob fresh ginger
- ½ cup chicken or vegetable stock
- 1 teaspoon cornstarch
- 1 tablespoon mirin
- 2 tablespoons sesame oil
- ½ teaspoon crushed red pepper
- 1½ pounds shrimp, peeled and deveined
- Kosher salt and freshly ground black pepper

shrimp fried rice with egg

1. Chop the leftover shrimp into bite-size pieces.

2. In a large nonstick pan, heat 1 tablespoon of the sesame oil over medium heat. Beat the eggs in a medium bowl and season with salt and pepper. When the oil is shimmering, add the eggs and scramble, 2 to 3 minutes. Remove from the pan and set aside.

3. Add the remaining 2 tablespoons sesame oil to the pan and heat over medium-high heat until shimmering. Add all the leftovers—chopped shrimp, vegetables, and rice—and cook, stirring, until warmed through and the rice is beginning to crisp, about 5 minutes. Drizzle with the soy sauce and return the eggs to the pan. Stir to combine, about 1 minute.

SERVES 2

Leftover shrimp and vegetable
 stir-fry
3 tablespoons sesame oil
2 large eggs
Leftover cooked rice
½ tablespoon soy sauce
Kosher salt and freshly ground
 black pepper

We have had more than one customer (Elana's mom included) turn the base for these turkey burgers into routine meals. After all, what's easier than ground turkey? Simple to mix up, this dish gets an unexpected boost of flavor from spinach, scallions, garlic, and cumin. It's ideal for making burgers or meatballs—both of which we share here—or anything else you can dream up!

SERVES 2 + 2 LEFTOVERS

2 cups baby spinach
4 scallions
4 cloves garlic
1 pound ground turkey
½ teaspoon ground cumin
1 tablespoon extra-virgin olive
   oil
¼ cup mayonnaise
½ lemon
2 hamburger buns
Kosher salt and freshly ground
   black pepper

1. Mince the spinach. Thinly slice the white and light green parts of the scallions. Mince the garlic.

2. In a large bowl, combine the turkey, spinach, scallions, half the garlic, and cumin. Season with salt and pepper and mix by hand until thoroughly combined. Divide the mixture in half. Form one half of the turkey mixture into 2 equal patties.

3. In a large pan, heat the olive oil over medium heat until shimmering. Add the patties and cook until golden on the bottom, about 5 minutes. Flip, cover, and cook until cooked through, about 6 minutes longer.

Use the remaining turkey mixture to form eight 1-inch meatballs. Cover with plastic wrap and refrigerate for up to 3 days. Alternatively, freeze in airtight containers for up to 1 month.

4. While the burgers cook, make the aioli. In a small bowl, whisk together the mayonnaise, remaining garlic, and juice of ½ lemon. Taste and add salt and pepper as needed.

5. Toast the buns cut-side down over medium heat in the pan used to cook the burgers, or in a toaster. Spread the aioli on the buns and top with the burgers. Serve hot.

spaghetti and turkey meatballs

SERVES 2

> 8 leftover turkey meatballs
> 8 ounces spaghetti
> ¼ cup basil pesto, store-bought
>   or homemade (page 39)
> Kosher salt

1. Preheat the oven to 425°F.

2. Bring a large pot of water to a boil over high heat for the pasta.

3. Arrange the turkey meatballs in a single layer on a baking sheet, spacing them evenly, and bake until cooked through, about 15 minutes.

4. While the meatballs bake, add the spaghetti and a generous pinch of salt to the boiling water. Cook until al dente according to the package instructions. Drain and toss with the pesto in a large bowl.

5. To serve, divide the pasta between 2 bowls and top with the meatballs.

roasted mustard-rubbed chicken

WITH ROOT VEGETABLE HASH

This Plated customer favorite incorporates a bunch of hearty root vegetables into a hash, making it a healthy, satisfying, and fun way to try vegetables you may never have cooked with—or tried—before (hi, rutabaga!). Cooked all in one pan, this dish is especially comforting and light on cleanup; but doubly comforting is knowing you have ready-made quesadilla fixins for the next day.

1. Preheat the oven to 425°F.

2. Peel the parsnip, carrots, celery root, and rutabaga (see page 229) and cut all into small dice. Pat the chicken dry.

3. Season the chicken on both sides with salt and pepper. Add skin-side down to a large ovenproof pan and place over medium-high heat. Cook without moving until the skin is browned and the fat is rendered, 6 to 8 minutes. Remove from the pan and set aside, skin-side up. Discard the fat from the pan.

4. While the chicken browns, strip the thyme leaves from the stems. Mince the rosemary leaves. Smash the garlic with the flat side of a knife and peel.

5. In a medium bowl, stir together the thyme, mustard, and 1 teaspoon of the olive oil to make a rub. Season with salt and pepper.

6. Return the pan used to cook the chicken to medium heat and add the remaining 1 tablespoon olive oil. Immediately add the parsnip, carrots, celery root, rutabaga, and garlic. Cook, stirring, until the vegetables begin to brown, about 5 minutes. Season with the rosemary and salt and pepper.

7. Spread the mustard rub over the chicken skin. Place the chicken skin-side up on top of the vegetables in the pan. Transfer to the oven and roast until the chicken is cooked through and the vegetables are tender, about 15 minutes.

8. Remove the chicken from the pan and set aside. Add the spinach to the vegetables and stir until wilted, about 1 minute. Taste and add salt and pepper as needed.

SERVES 2 + 2 LEFTOVERS

- 1 parsnip
- 2 carrots
- 1 pound celery root
- 6 ounces rutabaga
- 4 bone-in, skin-on chicken thighs
- 4 sprigs fresh thyme
- 2 sprigs fresh rosemary
- 3 cloves garlic
- 1 tablespoon Dijon mustard
- 1 tablespoon plus 1 teaspoon extra-virgin olive oil
- 2 cups baby spinach
- Kosher salt and freshly ground black pepper

> Set aside half the vegetables and chicken to use as leftovers. Let cool, then cover and store in the fridge for up to 4 days.

9. To serve, top the vegetables with the chicken.

LEFTOVERS

chicken and root vegetable quesadillas

SERVES 2

Leftover mustard-roasted
   chicken
Leftover roasted root
   vegetables
½ tablespoon ancho chile
   powder
4 6-inch flour or corn tortillas
½ cup shredded Jack cheese
1 tablespoon canola oil

1. Preheat the oven to 425°F.

2. Shred the chicken into bite-size pieces, discarding the skin and bones.

3. On a baking sheet, toss the leftover root vegetables with the ancho chile powder. Place in the oven and heat to warm through, about 10 minutes. Using the back of a fork, gently smash the vegetables until softened but still chunky.

4. Lay 2 tortillas flat on a clean, dry surface. Cover each tortilla with 2 tablespoons of Jack cheese, then layer the root vegetables and shredded chicken on top, dividing them evenly. Top each quesadilla with another 2 tablespoons of cheese and another tortilla. Press down lightly.

5. In a large pan, heat the canola oil over medium-high heat until shimmering. Add the quesadillas, working in batches if necessary, and cook until browned on the bottom, 2 to 3 minutes. Carefully flip and cook until the cheese is melted, about 2 minutes longer. Cut into quarters and serve hot.

spaghetti squash ragù

Spaghetti squash gets its name from the thin, pasta-like strands that are pulled out of it after roasting. Don't be fooled by its size; it makes an unexpectedly enormous amount of food—ideal for leftovers! This and the leftovers recipe are two of our favorite preparations, but there's ample opportunity for you to invent your own.

1. Preheat the oven to 450°F. Line a baking sheet with foil.

2. Halve the spaghetti squash lengthwise. Using a large spoon, scoop out and discard the seeds. Drizzle the cut sides with 1 tablespoon of the olive oil and season generously with salt and pepper. Arrange cut-side down on the lined baking sheet and roast until browning along the edges and very tender, about 35 minutes.

3. Meanwhile, in a large sauté pan, heat 1 tablespoon of the olive oil over medium-high heat. When the oil is shimmering, add the beef, season with salt and pepper, and cook, breaking it up with a wooden spoon, until the meat loses its color, 8 to 10 minutes. Using a slotted spoon, transfer the beef to a medium bowl and discard any liquid from the pan.

4. Meanwhile, halve the carrots lengthwise and slice them crosswise. Dice the onion. Strip the thyme leaves off the stems. Mince the garlic. Drain the tomatoes.

5. Heat the remaining 1 tablespoon olive oil in the same pan over medium-high heat. When the oil is shimmering, add the carrots, onion, thyme, garlic, crushed red pepper, and oregano. Sauté until the onion is soft and translucent, about 5 minutes. Return the meat to the pan. Add the tomato paste and stir to combine. Cook until brick red, about 2 minutes. Add the red wine and scrape up any browned bits from the bottom of the pan. Cook until reduced by half, about 2 minutes. Add the tomatoes and stock. Increase the heat to high and bring to a boil, then reduce the heat to medium and simmer until the ragù is thickened and the flavors are melded, about 15 minutes.

6. While the ragù simmers, when the spaghetti squash is cool enough to handle, use a large fork to pull and release the spaghetti-like strands into a large bowl.

SERVES 2 + 2 LEFTOVERS

- 2 small or 1 large spaghetti squash
- 3 tablespoons extra-virgin olive oil
- 1 pound ground beef
- 2 carrots
- 1 yellow onion
- 3 sprigs fresh thyme
- 3 cloves garlic
- 1 28-ounce can diced tomatoes
- ¼ teaspoon crushed red pepper
- 1 teaspoon dried oregano
- ½ tablespoon tomato paste
- ½ cup red wine
- 1 cup beef or chicken stock
- ¼ cup grated pecorino or Parmesan cheese
- Kosher salt and freshly ground black pepper

(recipe continues)

> Set aside half the shredded spaghetti squash to use as leftovers. Cover and refrigerate for up to 4 days.

7. Add the spaghetti squash to the ragù and stir to combine. Cook until warmed through and beginning to soak up the sauce, 2 to 3 minutes. Remove the pan from the heat and stir in the cheese. Taste and add salt and pepper as needed.

LEFTOVERS

spaghetti squash
with pine nuts and parmesan

SERVES 2

¼ cup pine nuts

3 cloves garlic

6 sprigs fresh flat-leaf parsley

⅛ teaspoon crushed red pepper

½ teaspoon dried oregano

Leftover shredded spaghetti squash

¼ cup chicken or vegetable stock

½ cup grated Parmesan cheese

2 tablespoons extra-virgin olive oil

Kosher salt and freshly ground black pepper

1. In a medium pan, spread out the pine nuts in a single layer and cook over medium heat, shaking the pan occasionally, until fragrant and toasted, about 5 minutes. Transfer the pine nuts to a small bowl.

2. Meanwhile, mince the garlic and roughly chop the parsley leaves.

3. In a large sauté pan, heat the olive oil over medium-high heat until shimmering. Add the garlic, crushed red pepper, and oregano. Cook, stirring, until fragrant, about 1 minute. Stir in the spaghetti squash and stock. Simmer until the pan is almost dry and the squash is warmed through, 3 to 5 minutes. Remove the pan from the heat and stir in the Parmesan. Taste and add salt and pepper as needed. Serve garnished with the toasted pine nuts and parsley.

make ahead

Plan-ahead chefs, rejoice! If your upcoming calendar doesn't leave much room for weeknight cooking, we've got you covered. Use this chapter to prepare for the days ahead on a Saturday or Sunday or whenever you do have time. These dishes might take a bit of extra time, but they're ideal for reheating—and taste even better a few days after cooking, if we're being honest. We've designed these recipes to yield 4 servings so that you can make your way through and enjoy them all week long. Our instructions tell you how to store them, but if you want to eat some right away—well, go right ahead!

beer-braised pulled chicken

WITH GUACAMOLE

The only thing that could compete with the fragrant, intoxicating smell of this braised chicken is the flavor of the oft-tested, perfect guacamole. Braising takes a little bit of work on the front end, but then requires almost no babysitting. Having rendered its contents incredibly tender, braised dishes always come out perfect, and this one leaves you with enough food for the week.

1. Roughly chop the chipotle chile and reserve 1 tablespoon of adobo sauce from the can. Halve and thinly slice the onion. Strip the oregano leaves from the stems. In a small bowl, stir together the paprika and cayenne.

2. In a large high-sided pan, heat the canola oil over medium-high heat. Rub the flesh sides of the chicken with the paprika mixture and season both sides with salt and pepper. When the oil is shimmering, add the chicken, flesh-side down, in a single layer. Sear until golden on the outside, 4 to 5 minutes per side. Remove to a plate.

3. Add the onion and oregano to the same pan over medium heat and cook until the onion is soft and translucent, about 5 minutes. Add the vinegar and Worcestershire sauce and cook until reduced by half, 1 to 2 minutes.

4. Add the brown sugar, crushed tomatoes, beer, chopped chipotle, and reserved adobo sauce and stir to combine. Increase the heat to high and bring to a boil, then return the chicken to the pan, nestling it in. Cover, reduce the heat to medium-low, and braise until the chicken is pulling away from the bone, about 1 hour.

5. Remove the chicken from the pan. Simmer the braising liquid, uncovered, over medium-high heat until reduced by half, about 10 minutes. Meanwhile, using 2 forks or tongs, shred the chicken meat into bite-size pieces, discarding the bones. Return the chicken to the reduced braising liquid and stir to combine.

SERVES 4

Chicken

- 1 chipotle pepper in adobo sauce (see Cheffy Nugget on page 54)
- 1 yellow onion
- 3 sprigs fresh oregano
- 1½ teaspoons sweet paprika
- ¼ teaspoon cayenne pepper
- 2 tablespoons canola oil
- 8 bone-in, skinless chicken thighs
- 3 tablespoons apple cider vinegar
- 1½ tablespoons Worcestershire sauce
- 1 tablespoon dark brown sugar
- 1 15-ounce can crushed tomatoes
- 1 12-ounce bottle lager-style beer

Kosher salt and freshly ground black pepper

(ingredients and recipe continue)

6. Halve the lime. Cut the tomato into ¼-inch dice. Finely dice the onion. Halve the jalapeño lengthwise, scrape out the seeds, and mince. Pick the cilantro leaves off the stems.

7. Halve the avocados and discard the pits. Cut a crosshatch pattern into the flesh, going all the way to the skin, then use a spoon to carefully scoop out the diced avocado into a medium bowl.

8. Add the tomato, onion, jalapeño, cilantro, and hot sauce to the avocado. Squeeze in the lime juice and gently toss. Taste and add salt as needed. Transfer to an airtight container. Press plastic wrap down over the guacamole, then cover and store for up to 4 days. Allow the chicken to cool completely and store in the fridge for up to 4 days. Alternatively, transfer portions of the chicken to airtight containers and freeze for up to 1 month. To reheat, place the desired amount with sauce in a medium pot and warm, covered, over medium heat.

9. Serve the guacamole alongside the chicken.

Guacamole

1 lime
1 small vine-ripe tomato
½ small red onion
½ jalapeño
6 sprigs fresh cilantro
2 avocados
A few dashes hot sauce
 (we like Cholula)
Kosher salt

brown sugar–braised short ribs

The most difficult part about making short ribs is waiting for them to be ready to eat. That's why we've included them in this chapter; the long wait happens way before "hanger" (angry hunger) kicks in. Just be patient—the slow braise is definitely worth it! The brown sugar, red wine, and veal stock create the perfect match of caramelized meat and flavorful sauce.

1. Preheat the oven to 350°F.

2. Dice the onion. Slice the carrots and celery on a diagonal. Roughly chop the shallots. Lightly smash the garlic with the flat side of a knife and peel.

3. In a large Dutch oven, heat the canola oil over medium heat. Rub the meaty parts of the short ribs with half the brown sugar. Season generously on both sides with salt and pepper. When the oil is shimmering, add the short ribs in a single layer (work in batches if necessary), meat-side down, and sear until well browned and beginning to caramelize, about 5 minutes. Remove to a plate and set aside.

4. Add the onion, carrots, celery, shallots, and garlic to the pan. Season lightly with salt and pepper and cook until softening, 6 to 7 minutes. Add the Worcestershire sauce and vinegar and scrape up any browned bits from the bottom of the pan.

5. Return the short ribs to the pan meat-side up and pour the red wine and veal stock over them. The short ribs should be about two-thirds submerged; nestle them into the vegetables if needed. Add the bay leaf, thyme, and remaining brown sugar. Increase the heat to high and bring to a boil, then cover the pan and transfer it to the oven. Braise until the short ribs are tender but not yet falling apart, about 2 hours.

6. Uncover the ribs and flip meat-side down. Return the pan to the oven, uncovered, and continue braising for 30 minutes, then flip once again. Continue braising, uncovered, until the short ribs are fork-tender and well caramelized, about 30 minutes longer. Allow the ribs and braising liquid to cool completely, then refrigerate for up to 4 days. Alternatively, transfer portions to airtight containers and freeze for up to 1 month. To reheat the ribs, preheat the oven to 350°F. Scrape off and discard any fat from the surface of the liquid, then heat in the pan, covered, until warmed through.

SERVES 4

- 1 small yellow onion
- 2 carrots
- 1 stalk celery
- 2 shallots
- 5 cloves garlic
- 2 tablespoons canola oil
- 5 pounds bone-in short ribs
- ⅓ cup packed light brown sugar
- 1 tablespoon Worcestershire sauce
- 1 tablespoon balsamic vinegar
- 1½ cups red wine
- 1½ cups veal stock
- 1 bay leaf
- 6 sprigs fresh thyme
- Kosher salt and freshly ground black pepper

CHEFFY NUGGET: Short ribs are actually best when they've had time to rest in their braising liquid—the meat absorbs the surrounding delicious juices as it cools. One of the perks of making them ahead is that during refrigeration, the fat from the sauce congeals and turns orange on top of the braising liquid, making it much easier to scrape off and discard.

slow-simmered turkey chili

WITH POBLANO, WHITE BEANS, AND BAKED TORTILLA CHIPS

Lighter than beef chili, our turkey version has the perfect amount of spice that builds as you make your way through a bowl. Plus, homemade tortilla chips (and a handful of Cheddar cheese) make everything better. This dish is excellent to make on a Sunday night in winter and save to warm you up when you can't bear to leave the house.

1. Preheat the oven to 425°F.

2. In a large pot, heat 1 tablespoon of the olive oil over medium heat. When the oil is shimmering, add the turkey and season with salt and pepper. Cook the turkey, breaking it up with a wooden spoon as it browns, for about 10 minutes.

3. Meanwhile, halve the poblanos lengthwise, discard the seeds, and slice. Mince the onions and garlic. Drain and rinse the white beans. Cut each tortilla into 8 wedges.

4. Add the poblanos, onions, and garlic to the turkey and cook until the onions are soft and translucent, about 5 minutes. Stir in the cumin, oregano, and chili powder. Cook until fragrant, about 1 minute. Stir in the beans and stock. Increase the heat to high and bring to a boil, then reduce the heat to medium and simmer until thickened, 30 to 40 minutes.

5. While the chili simmers, toss the tortilla wedges on a baking sheet with the remaining 1 tablespoon olive oil. Arrange them in a single layer and season with salt. Bake until golden and crisp, about 15 minutes.

6. Add the milk to the thickened chili, stir to combine, and increase the heat to medium-high. Simmer until thickened further and warmed through, 4 to 5 minutes. Taste and add salt and pepper as needed. Allow the chili to cool completely, then refrigerate for up to 4 days. Alternatively, transfer in portions to airtight containers and freeze for up to 1 month. To reheat the chili, place the desired amount in a medium pot and warm, covered, over medium heat. Keep the tortilla chips in an airtight container at room temperature until ready to serve, up to 2 days.

7. Before serving, dice the tomatoes. Serve the chili hot, garnished with the tomato, Cheddar, and tortilla chips.

SERVES 4

- 2 tablespoons extra-virgin olive oil
- 1½ pounds ground turkey
- 2 poblano chiles
- 2 yellow onions
- 2 cloves garlic
- 2 cups canned white beans
- 6 corn tortillas
- 2 teaspoons ground cumin
- 2 teaspoons dried oregano
- 2 teaspoons chili powder
- 4 cups chicken stock
- 1 cup whole milk
- 2 plum or vine-riped tomatoes
- ½ cup shredded Cheddar cheese
- Kosher salt and freshly ground black pepper

braised harissa lamb shanks

WITH COUSCOUS AND HERB SALAD

When faced with a last-minute, large-scale catering event, instead of panicking, we dreamed up this dish as the ideal way to feed—and please—a big crowd. When guests came looking for seconds, we knew it was a keeper. These lamb shanks are roasted, then braised for a perfect brown crust on the exterior with incredibly tender meat underneath.

1. Preheat the oven to 475°F.

2. Halve the garlic heads horizontally. Season the lamb generously with salt and pepper, then rub harissa all over and arrange in a large Dutch oven or baking dish. Scatter over the garlic, thyme, and rosemary. Roast, uncovered, until the lamb is beginning to brown, about 20 minutes. Remove and reduce the oven temperature to 350°F.

3. Pour the white wine over the lamb, cover the Dutch oven or pan, and return to the oven to braise until very tender, about 2 hours 15 minutes. Once tender, uncover, add 2 cups of the chicken stock, and braise, uncovered, for another 30 minutes to allow the pan juices to reduce.

4. When the lamb is almost done braising, mince the shallot. Pick the mint, parsley, and cilantro leaves and place in a bowl. Halve the lemon.

5. In a medium sauté pan, heat 1 tablespoon of the olive oil over medium heat until shimmering. Add the shallot and cook until soft and translucent, about 2 minutes. Add the couscous and toast, stirring, for about 2 minutes. Add the remaining 2 cups chicken stock and simmer until the liquid is absorbed and the couscous is tender, 10 to 12 minutes. Taste and add salt and pepper as needed.

> Allow the lamb to cool, then shred the meat, discarding the bones. Store portions with any juices in airtight containers in the fridge for up to 4 days. To reheat, add to a medium pot and warm, covered, over medium heat. Store the couscous, herbs, and lemon separately. To reheat the couscous, place in a medium pan over medium heat and warm through.

6. Squeeze the lemon over the herbs, add the remaining 1 tablespoon olive oil, and toss to coat. Serve the lamb with the couscous and herb salad alongside.

SERVES 4

- 2 **heads garlic**
- 4 **lamb shanks (about 6 pounds total)**
- ½ cup **harissa paste**
- 8 **sprigs fresh thyme**
- 4 **sprigs fresh rosemary**
- 1 **750ml bottle white wine (we like Pinot Grigio)**
- 4 cups **chicken stock**
- 1 **shallot**
- 1 **bunch fresh mint**
- ¼ **bunch fresh flat-leaf parsley**
- ¼ **bunch fresh cilantro**
- 1 **lemon**
- 2 tablespoons **extra-virgin olive oil**
- 1 cup **Israeli couscous**
- **Kosher salt and freshly ground black pepper**

white lasagna

WITH BUTTERNUT SQUASH, KALE, AND MUSHROOMS

Lasagna is our go-to comfort food to make for anyone having a bad day. Maybe you need some on a rainy Monday, or maybe a friend could use a batch. Like all perfect make-ahead meals, it just keeps getting better and better. We love this creamy béchamel paired with these earthy vegetables.

1. Preheat the oven to 425°F.

2. Quarter the mushrooms. Peel the squash and cut it into ½-inch pieces. On a baking sheet, toss the mushrooms and squash with 2 tablespoons of the olive oil and salt and pepper. Arrange in a single layer and roast until tender, about 18 minutes.

3. While the vegetables roast, strip the stems from the kale leaves, then cut the leaves into bite-size pieces. Thinly slice the garlic.

4. In a large pan, heat the remaining 1 tablespoon olive oil over medium heat until shimmering. Add the kale and garlic and cook until the kale is wilted and bright green, about 4 minutes. Season with salt and pepper and set aside.

5. Remove the roasted mushrooms and squash from the oven and reduce the oven temperature to 400°F. Using a fork or the back of a spoon, mash the squash.

6. To make the béchamel, in a medium saucepan, melt the butter over medium heat. When the butter is foamy, sprinkle in the flour and whisk until the mixture is smooth and golden, about 2 minutes. Slowly pour in the milk, whisking continuously until no lumps remain. Simmer, stirring occasionally, until the sauce is thick and coats the back of the spoon, 6 to 7 minutes. Season with the nutmeg, salt, and pepper. Add ¼ cup of the Parmesan, stir to combine, and remove the pot from the heat.

7. Spread a thin layer of the béchamel over the bottom of a 9 x 13-inch baking dish. Add a layer of lasagna noodles, followed by a layer of squash and mushrooms, then kale, then more béchamel, and a sprinkle of Parmesan. Repeat to make 2 more layers: noodles, vegetables, béchamel, and Parmesan. Top with a final layer of noodles and the remaining béchamel. Sprinkle with the remaining Parmesan and the Gruyère.

SERVES 4

- 8 ounces cremini mushrooms
- 1 pound butternut squash
- 3 tablespoons extra-virgin olive oil, plus more for drizzling
- 2 bunches lacinato kale
- 2 cloves garlic
- 8 tablespoons (1 stick) unsalted butter
- ½ cup all-purpose flour
- 4 cups whole milk
- ⅛ teaspoon ground nutmeg
- 1 cup grated Parmesan cheese
- 2 9-ounce boxes no-boil lasagna noodles
- ½ cup shredded Gruyère cheese
- Kosher salt and freshly ground black pepper

8. Loosely cover the pan with foil, transfer to the oven, and bake until the lasagna is bubbling, about 30 minutes. Increase the oven temperature to 450°F. Uncover the lasagna and continue baking until golden, about 10 minutes longer.

9. Remove from the oven and allow to cool completely before cutting into pieces.

10. Wrap with foil and store in the fridge for up to 5 days, or in the freezer for up to 1 month. To reheat, microwave the lasagna or warm it, covered, in the oven at 350°F.

two-hour bolognese

WITH HOMEMADE PASTA RAGS

Fresh pasta from scratch seems daunting, but in reality it's much easier than you imagine—and only takes three ingredients! You'll have plenty of time to perfect your pasta kneading and folding technique while your rich and silky Bolognese simmers away.

1. Halve the carrots and celery lengthwise, then slice crosswise. Dice the onion. Drain the tomatoes. Lightly smash the garlic with the flat side of a knife and peel. Leave 2 cloves whole and mince 2 cloves.

2. In a large pot, heat 2 tablespoons of the olive oil over medium-high heat until shimmering. Add the carrots, celery, onion, and minced garlic and cook until very soft, about 10 minutes. Remove to a plate and set aside.

3. Heat another 1 tablespoon of the olive oil in the same pot over medium heat until shimmering. Add the smashed garlic cloves and cook until golden, about 2 minutes. Remove and discard. Add the veal, pork, and beef and season well with salt and pepper. Cook, breaking it up with a wooden spoon, until the meat loses its color and the liquid is mostly evaporated, about 10 minutes. Add the tomato paste, stir to combine, and cook until brick red, about 2 minutes.

4. Add the white wine and bring to a simmer. Cook until reduced by three-fourths, about 5 minutes. Add the tomatoes, stock, thyme, and sautéed vegetables. Increase the heat to high and bring to a boil, then reduce the heat to low and simmer, stirring occasionally, until the sauce is thickened and most of the liquid has been absorbed, about 1 hour 30 minutes.

5. When the Bolognese is thick, add the milk, increase the heat to medium, and simmer until the milk is completely absorbed and the sauce is thickened, about 15 minutes longer. Taste and add salt and pepper as needed.

SERVES 4

Bolognese
- 2 carrots
- 1 stalk celery
- 1 yellow onion
- 1 15-ounce can diced tomatoes
- 4 cloves garlic
- 3 tablespoons extra-virgin olive oil
- 8 ounces ground veal
- 8 ounces ground pork
- 8 ounces ground beef
- 2 tablespoons tomato paste
- 1 cup white wine
- 4 cups beef or chicken stock
- 4 sprigs fresh thyme
- 1½ cups whole milk
- Kosher salt and freshly ground black pepper

Pasta Rags
- 2 cups all-purpose flour, plus more for dusting
- 3 large eggs
- 2 large egg yolks
- 3 tablespoons extra-virgin olive oil
- Kosher salt

Allow the Bolognese to cool completely, then divide it into portions and store in airtight containers in the fridge for up to 4 days or freeze for up to 1 month. To reheat, place the desired amount in a medium pan over medium heat to warm through.

6. In a large bowl, whisk together the flour and ½ teaspoon salt. Make a well in the center and add the whole eggs, egg yolks, and 1 tablespoon of the olive oil. Using your hands, begin to incorporate the flour into the yolks, mixing until thoroughly combined. Turn out the dough onto a dry, lightly floured surface. Using your hands, knead until smooth and elastic, 5 to 10 minutes. Wrap the dough in plastic and refrigerate for at least 30 minutes and up to 1 hour.

7. Bring a large pot of water to a boil over high heat for the pasta.

8. Return the ball of dough to a lightly dusted surface and cut into 1-inch-wide slabs. Working with one slab at a time, flatten with a rolling pin and stretch, then fold, letter-style, into thirds. Roll out with a rolling pin until almost paper thin. Cut the sheets into 1-inch-wide strips and arrange in a single layer on a flour-dusted baking sheet as they're finished.

9. Add the rags and a generous pinch of salt to the boiling water. Cook until just al dente, about 4 minutes. Drain, drizzle with the remaining 2 tablespoons olive oil, then allow to cool completely. Store in an airtight container in the refrigerator for up to 4 days.

10. To reheat, add the Bolognese to a medium sauté pan over medium heat and cook to warm through. When the Bolognese is hot, add the pasta rags and stir to warm through. Taste and add salt and pepper as needed.

weekend feasts

If you're a person who sees the weekend as the perfect opportunity for an all-day braise, 1) Give us a call! Let's hang out! and 2) Read on, because this chapter is especially dedicated to you. These are more ambitious recipes that take a little extra time and a little extra love, but they present a very rewarding opportunity to expand your culinary repertoire. They're designed to make 4 to 6 servings so that you can share your weekend achievements with a crowd of your hungriest friends.

spinach and goat cheese frittata

WITH GRUYÈRE AND THYME BISCUITS

Elaborate breakfast spreads were a weekend staple in Suzanne's house growing up. Always on the menu? Biscuits! This cheesy, herby version is a slightly more refined approach to breakfast-for-dinner. (Although isn't the smell of breakfast truly welcome any time of the day?)

1. Strip the thyme leaves from the stems. Finely chop the rosemary leaves. In a large bowl, whisk together the thyme, rosemary, flour, Gruyère, baking powder, baking soda, and ¾ teaspoon salt. Cut the butter into small pieces or grate the butter on the large holes of a box grater. Add to the flour and, using your fingers, work the butter into the flour, creating a coarse meal with lumps no larger than peas.

2. In a medium bowl, whisk together the yogurt, sugar, and milk. Slowly add the wet mixture to the dry and combine to create a shaggy dough. Set aside.

3. Preheat the broiler to high. Roughly chop the spinach. Halve the onion and thinly slice. Thinly slice the chives. In a large bowl, whisk together the eggs, milk, and chives. Season with salt and pepper and whisk again.

4. In a medium cast iron skillet or ovenproof pan, heat the olive oil over medium-high heat until shimmering. Add the onion and cook until very soft and beginning to caramelize, 8 to 10 minutes.

5. When the onion is caramelized, add half the goat cheese to the bowl with the eggs and whisk until frothy.

6. Add the spinach to the skillet and cook until just wilted, about 1 minute. Turn the heat to medium-low and pour the egg mixture over the vegetables. Stir to combine and continue stirring, slowly, until the eggs are almost set. Remove the pan from the heat.

7. Sprinkle the remaining goat cheese over the frittata and immediately transfer the pan to the top rack of the oven. Broil until the frittata is puffed and golden, about 5 minutes. Remove and set aside while you bake the biscuits; the frittata may sink slightly.

SERVES 4 TO 6

Biscuit Dough
- 4 sprigs fresh thyme
- 1 sprig fresh rosemary
- 1½ cups all-purpose flour
- 1 cup shredded Gruyère cheese
- 1 teaspoon baking powder
- ½ teaspoon baking soda
- 5 tablespoons cold unsalted butter
- ½ cup Greek yogurt
- 1 tablespoon sugar
- ½ cup milk
- Kosher salt

Frittata
- 2 cups spinach
- 1 Vidalia onion
- 6 fresh chives
- 9 extra-large eggs
- ¼ cup whole milk
- 2 tablespoons extra-virgin olive oil
- ¾ cup crumbled goat cheese
- Kosher salt and freshly ground black pepper

- 1 extra-large egg
- 1 cup microgreens or baby lettuce
- 1 tablespoon extra-virgin olive oil
- Kosher salt and freshly ground black pepper

8. Reduce the oven temperature to 400°F. Turn out the biscuit dough onto a lightly floured surface and pat it into an even 2-inch-thick rectangle. Using a cookie cutter or the rim of a drinking glass, cut the dough into 2- to 3-inch rounds. Reroll the scraps to get the most out of your dough (no biscuit left behind!). Place on a baking sheet, spaced 2 inches apart, and bake until golden, about 18 minutes. Meanwhile, in a small bowl, beat the egg. After 18 minutes, brush the top of each biscuit with beaten egg, then return to the oven and bake for 2 minutes longer. Remove and set aside to cool for about 5 minutes.

9. While the biscuits cool, in a medium bowl, toss the microgreens with the olive oil and salt and pepper.

10. To serve, cut the frittata into slices and garnish with the greens. Serve the biscuits alongside.

CHEFFY NUGGET: The trick to ultra-fluffy, "layered" biscuits is grating cold butter into the flour. The shreds of butter melt during baking, creating pockets of air that result in the ultimate biscuit texture.

dim sum

PORK AND CHIVE SHUMAI, TOFU-SCALLION DUMPLINGS, AND SHRIMP GYOZA

Dim sum is a Chinese tasting of small bites—perfect for the eater who wants to try a little bit of everything. Here, we've featured some of our favorite dumplings (because what's better than a bite wrapped in dough?). Our best advice for making an array of homemade dumplings is to enlist a friend to help you seal wonton wrappers. Give them a "sous chef" title—and a glass of sake—and you've cut your labor in half.

1. Make the dipping sauce: Thinly slice the Thai chile. In a medium bowl, mix together the soy sauce, Thai chile, vinegar, sesame oil, and crushed red pepper. Whisk to combine and set aside.

2. Make the dim sum: Mince the garlic and ginger. Divide the ginger and garlic evenly among 3 medium bowls, one for each type of dim sum.

3. Make the shumai filling: Thinly slice the chives, mince the scallions, and add them to one of the bowls. Add the pork and season with salt and pepper. Mix by hand.

4. Make the dumpling filling: Discard the shiitake stems and mince the caps. Mince the scallions. Finely chop the tofu. Add the mushrooms, tofu, and scallions to another one of the bowls. Season with salt and pepper and mix by hand.

5. Make the gyoza filling: Finely chop the spinach and shrimp and add to the last bowl. Add the oyster sauce, season with salt and pepper, and mix by hand.

6. To assemble all the dumplings, fill a small bowl with warm water. One at a time, lay the wonton wrappers on a clean, dry surface and place a heaping teaspoon of filling in the center. Using your finger, rub warm water around the outer edge of the wrapper.

7. For the pork shumai, pinch up the sides of the wrapper to come together over the filling, leaving a tiny bit of the filling exposed at the top. For the tofu dumplings, pinch the edges together over the filling in a four-pronged star shape. For the shrimp gyoza, fold the wrapper over the filling and pinch all around, making small pleats to seal.

SERVES 4 TO 6

Dipping Sauce
1 fresh red Thai chile
½ cup soy sauce
¼ cup rice vinegar
2 tablespoons sesame oil
¼ teaspoon crushed red pepper

Dim Sum
3 cloves garlic
1½-inch knob fresh ginger

Shumai Filling
½ bunch fresh chives
1½ scallions
4 ounces ground pork

Dumpling Filling
2 ounces shiitake mushrooms
1½ scallions
2 ounces tofu

Gyoza Filling
½ cup baby spinach
4 ounces shrimp, shelled and deveined
1 tablespoon oyster sauce

1 package 3- to 4-inch round wonton wrappers
1 tablespoon sesame oil
Kosher salt and freshly ground black pepper

8. To cook the pork shumai: In a medium pot, bring 1 inch of water to a boil over high heat. Set a steamer basket or colander over the pot (if using a colander, be sure it isn't touching the water). Add the dumplings in a single layer, then cover tightly with a lid and steam until the wrappers are translucent and tender, 6 to 8 minutes.

9. To cook the tofu-scallion dumplings and shrimp gyoza: In a large pan, heat the sesame oil over medium-high heat until shimmering. Add the dumplings in a single layer, working in batches if necessary, and cook without moving until browned on the bottom, 2 to 3 minutes. Add ¼ cup water and cover the pan. Steam until the wrappers are translucent and tender, 3 to 4 minutes.

10. Serve the dim sum with the dipping sauce alongside.

CHEFFY NUGGET: Keep the "wonton wrappers in waiting" covered with a damp towel so they don't dry out. Do the same with the prepared dumplings you haven't yet cooked.

buttermilk-brined fried chicken,

CHEDDAR CORNBREAD, AND HOT PEPPER JELLY

It might sound like an unconventional combination, but a buttermilk and pickle juice brine results in some of the tastiest fried chicken you'll ever eat. Coated in Old Bay–seasoned flour and drizzled with honey right out of the pan, this chicken is spicy, sweet, and leaves nothing to be desired—except seconds. Plan ahead to get the most out of this dish. The longer the chicken brines (at least 2 hours), the better—and the hot pepper jelly needs at least 4 hours chilling time to maximize its flavor in prep, but you can make it a few days in advance.

1. Cut the bell peppers into ¼-inch dice. Cut the onion into small dice. Seed and mince the chiles. In a large bowl, combine the bell peppers, onion, and chiles. Season generously with salt and toss to combine well. Cover with plastic wrap and chill in the fridge for at least 4 hours or overnight.

2. Drain and rinse the vegetables well and transfer to a medium pot. Add the vinegar, water, sugar, and mustard seeds and bring to a boil over high heat. Once the sugar is dissolved, reduce the heat to medium-high and simmer until the mixture is saucy with the consistency of a relish. Remove the pot from the heat and allow to cool completely, about 30 minutes. If not using right away, transfer to an airtight container and store in the fridge for up to 5 days.

3. Roughly chop the jalapeños. In a large container or bowl, combine the jalapeños, buttermilk, pickle juice, rosemary sprigs, and hot sauce to make the brine. Add the chicken, being sure to submerge. Cover with a tight-fitting lid or plastic wrap and refrigerate for at least 2 hours and up to 48 hours.

4. In a large bowl, whisk together the flour, Old Bay, paprika, and cayenne. Season generously with salt and black pepper. Working with one piece at a time, remove the chicken from the brine, allowing the excess to drip off, then add to the flour mixture and turn to coat. Remove, shake off any excess, and transfer to a large plate. Set the dredged chicken aside to come to room temperature while you bake the cornbread.

5. Preheat the oven to 375°F.

SERVES 4 TO 6

Pepper Jelly
- 2 red bell peppers
- 1 green bell pepper
- 1 white onion
- 1 serrano chile
- 2 Fresno or cherry pepper chiles
- 1 cup apple cider vinegar
- 1 cup water
- ¾ cup sugar
- 1 tablespoon mustard seeds
- Kosher salt

Chicken
- 2 jalapeños
- 2 quarts buttermilk
- A few splashes pickle juice from a pickle jar
- 4 sprigs fresh rosemary
- ½ tablespoon hot sauce (we like Tabasco)
- 5 bone-in, skin-on chicken thighs
- 5 skin-on chicken drumsticks
- 2 cups all-purpose flour

(ingredients and recipe continue)

6. Thinly slice the scallions. Add to a large bowl along with the cornmeal, flour, baking powder, sugar, and 2 teaspoons salt. Stir to combine. In a medium bowl, whisk together the eggs, milk, and honey until smooth. While whisking, slowly add the wet ingredients to the dry just until combined. Gently stir in the Cheddar.

7. Place the butter in a medium ovenproof skillet or baking dish and place in the oven until the pan is hot and the butter is melted, about 5 minutes. Remove from the oven and pour the melted butter into the batter, gently stirring to combine. Immediately pour the batter back into the hot pan and return it to the oven. Bake until golden on top and just set, 30 to 35 minutes.

8. While the cornbread bakes, fill a large sauté pan or Dutch oven halfway with canola oil (you may not need the full quart). Heat over medium heat until a deep-fry thermometer reads 350° to 370°F.

9. Working in batches, without overcrowding the pot, add the chicken to the oil and fry until the crust is golden and the juices run clear inside, 3 to 4 minutes per side for smaller pieces, and about 5 minutes per side for larger. Keep a close eye on your oil; if it starts smoking, turn the heat down. If it's not bubbling around your chicken, turn the heat up slightly. As soon as the chicken is cooked, transfer it to a large baking sheet lined with paper towels to drain and immediately sprinkle with salt, then drizzle with the honey.

10. Serve the fried chicken with the cornbread and the hot pepper jelly alongside to spoon over both.

3 tablespoons Old Bay seasoning
2 teaspoons sweet paprika
½ teaspoon cayenne pepper
1 quart canola oil, for frying
2 tablespoons honey
Kosher salt and freshly ground black pepper

Cornbread
4 scallions
1½ cups cornmeal
¾ cup all-purpose flour
1½ teaspoons baking powder
2 tablespoons sugar
5 large eggs
1½ cups whole milk
¼ cup honey
¾ cup shredded Cheddar cheese
8 tablespoons (1 stick) unsalted butter
Kosher salt

CHEFFY NUGGET: A deep-fry thermometer is essential to this recipe. Monitoring your oil temperature will help you stay in that sweet spot around 350°F. Oil that's too hot will burn the outside of your chicken before cooking the inside, and oil that's too cold won't crisp the skin properly. Keep in mind that the oil will cool slightly when you add the chicken, so be sure to allow it to return to the proper temperature in between batches.

pork shoyu ramen

Ramen, a steaming bowl of Japanese broth with chewy noodles and a pile of garnish, is incomparably satisfying on a freezing-cold day. We made this recipe doable at home, but still with authentic Japanese flavors, so you may need to plan a trip to your local Asian market in advance. This isn't a condensed recipe—but after 2 days of cooking, you'll feel duly rewarded with both a belly full of restaurant-quality ramen and the highest praise from your fellow diners. The broth is definitely the star here, but if you're looking for a shortcut, you can ask your local butcher. We don't recommend using store-bought broth, though—you're better off getting takeout in that case!

1. Quarter the leeks lengthwise and cut crosswise into 2-inch pieces. Place in a bowl of cold water and allow the dirt to sink to the bottom. Peel the ginger. Roughly chop the mushrooms. Pat the pork dry and season all over with salt and pepper. Pat the chicken dry.

2. In a large pot, heat the canola oil over medium heat until shimmering. Add the pork and brown on all sides, about 12 minutes total. Add the water and scrape up any browned bits. Drain the leeks and add to the pan along with the chicken, ginger, chopped mushrooms, garlic, and dark soy sauce. Bring to a boil, cover, then reduce the heat to medium-low and simmer for 1 hour. Uncover, flip the pork, and continue to simmer, uncovered, until tender, about 1 hour longer. Periodically skim off any foam.

3. Remove the pork to a platter to cool slightly, about 30 minutes. Wrap tightly in plastic and refrigerate overnight.

4. Strain the broth and discard all the solids. Return the broth to the pot and bring to a boil over high heat. Add the kombu, cover, and simmer for 1 hour 30 minutes.

5. Uncover the broth, discard the kombu, and add the light soy sauce, sake, and mirin.

6. Remove the pot from the heat and allow to cool, 30 minutes to 1 hour. Cover and transfer to the fridge to chill overnight.

SERVES 4 TO 6

Broth

- 2 leeks
- 3 large knobs fresh ginger
- 6 ounces shiitake mushrooms
- 4 pounds boneless pork butt (shoulder), tied
- 3 pounds chicken bones or wings
- 1 tablespoon canola oil
- 6 quarts water
- 6 cloves garlic
- ½ cup dark soy sauce
- 1 sheet kombu
- ⅓ cup light soy sauce
- 1½ tablespoons sake
- 1 tablespoon mirin
- Kosher salt and freshly ground black pepper

(ingredients and recipe continue)

7. When you're ready to serve, remove the pot from the fridge and skim off any fat from the top. Return the pot to high heat and bring to a boil, then reduce the heat to medium-high and simmer for 1 hour. Taste and add salt as needed.

8. When the broth is almost done simmering, prepare the garnishes: Preheat the broiler to high. Bring a large pot of water to a boil over high heat for the ramen.

9. Place the eggs in a medium pot and cover with cold water. Bring to a boil, then cover, and set aside for 5 minutes. Remove the eggs and immediately transfer to a bowl of ice water to stop the cooking, about 5 minutes. Peel the eggs.

10. Meanwhile, unwrap the pork and place it on a baking sheet. Broil until the outside is crisp and golden, about 12 minutes.

11. While the pork is broiling, finely chop the shiitake mushroom caps (discard the stems). In a small pan, heat the sesame oil over medium heat until shimmering. Add the mushrooms and cook until golden brown, about 8 minutes.

12. When the water comes to a boil, add the ramen and a generous pinch of salt and cook according to the package instructions. Drain the ramen.

13. Cut the pork crosswise into ¼-inch slices. Thinly slice the scallions on a diagonal. Break the nori into 1-inch pieces. Halve the eggs. Divide the ramen among 6 bowls. Place a few slices of pork on top. Ladle over the hot broth, then garnish with the eggs, scallions, mushrooms, fermented bamboo shoots, and nori. Add Sriracha to taste.

Garnishes and Ramen
- 6 large eggs
- 4 ounces shiitake mushrooms
- 1 teaspoon sesame oil
- 6 individual packages fresh ramen noodles
- 6 scallions
- 3 sheets nori
- ½ cup fermented bamboo shoots
- 1 tablespoon Sriracha sauce (optional)
- Kosher salt

CHEFFY NUGGET: Soft-boiling eggs is an exact science: To get the perfect soft yolk, set a timer for exactly 5 minutes once the water starts boiling. When it is finished, transfer to ice water immediately after to stop the cooking.

roasted peking duck

WITH SWEET CHILE EGGPLANT

Peking duck is a near-perfect food in our opinion: tender meat, crispy skin, and sweet-and-tangy hoisin sauce, all wrapped up in a warm pancake. Roasting duck legs rather than the whole bird, as a restaurant would, cuts the cook time and mess way down. Call around to your local butchers and grocery stores to see if they have duck legs in stock (your usual grocer may not always carry them); they can often be ordered with advance notice. But trust us—this food adventure is one worth going on.

1. Preheat the oven to 400°F.

2. Rub the duck legs all over with the Chinese 5-spice powder. Season with salt. Working in batches if necessary, place the duck skin-side down in a large ovenproof pan over medium heat. Cook without moving until the fat has rendered and the skin is beginning to crisp, 10 to 12 minutes. Remove the duck from the pan and carefully pour off and discard the excess fat.

3. Return the duck skin-side up to the pan and transfer it to the oven. Roast until the meat begins to pull off the bone, about 1 hour, carefully pouring off any rendered fat about halfway through.

4. While the duck roasts, peel the cucumbers and cut into 2-inch-long spears. Cut the white and light green parts of the scallions into 2-inch pieces, then quarter the pieces lengthwise into strips.

5. When the duck is almost done roasting, make the sweet chile eggplant: Quarter the eggplants lengthwise, then cut them crosswise into 1-inch pieces. In a large pan, heat the sesame oil and canola oil over medium-high heat until shimmering. Add the eggplant and cook, stirring, until golden brown and crisping, 12 to 15 minutes.

6. While the eggplant cooks, stack the tortillas and wrap them in foil. Place in the oven along with the duck to warm for 10 to 20 minutes.

SERVES 4 TO 6

Peking Duck
8 duck legs
¼ cup Chinese 5-spice powder
2 English cucumbers
2 bunches scallions
Kosher salt

Sweet Chile Eggplant
2 pounds Chinese or Japanese eggplant
1 tablespoon sesame oil
1 tablespoon canola oil
1 tablespoon sambal oelek
½ cup chicken stock
3 tablespoons soy sauce
1 tablespoon rice vinegar
1 tablespoon light brown sugar
1 tablespoon cornstarch
Kosher salt and freshly ground black pepper

½ cup hoisin sauce, for serving
1 package 8-inch flour tortillas

7. In a medium bowl, whisk together the sambal oelek, chicken stock, soy sauce, vinegar, and brown sugar. Remove the crisped eggplant to a plate. Reduce the heat to medium and add the sambal oelek mixture. Bring to a simmer, then whisk in the cornstarch and cook until the sauce is thickened, about 1 minute. Return the eggplant and stir to coat. Remove the pan from the heat and taste and add salt and pepper as needed.

8. Transfer the roasted duck to a plate to rest for about 5 minutes. Then pull the meat off the bones and shred or cut into 1-inch slices.

9. To serve, spread a dollop of hoisin sauce over each pancake, then top with duck, cucumber, and scallions. Serve with the eggplant alongside.

7. Stir in the wine, vinegar, and both sugars. Bring to a simmer, then cook, stirring occasionally, until sticky and caramelized, about 15 minutes longer. Remove the pan from the heat and allow to cool to room temperature, about 15 minutes. Taste and add salt and black pepper as needed. Set aside.

8. When the bread pudding has soaked, pour over the remaining milk mixture. It should be mostly submerged, with some bread poking out through the custard. Bake until the custard is set and the bread is deep golden, about 1 hour. Set aside to cool. Leave the oven on, but increase the oven temperature to 425°F for the steak.

9. In a medium pan, heat the olive oil over medium-high heat. Pat the steak dry and season generously on both sides with salt and pepper. When the oil is shimmering, add the steak and sear, without moving, until well browned, about 4 minutes per side. Transfer the pan to the oven and cook until medium-rare, 3 to 5 minutes. Immediately transfer the steak to a large cutting board or plate, top with the butter and whole thyme sprigs, and allow to rest for 5 to 10 minutes.

10. Slice the steak against the grain. Serve family-style with the red onion jam for spooning on top and the bread pudding alongside.

Steak

- 1 tablespoon extra-virgin olive oil
- 1½ pounds New York strip steak (about 1 inch thick)
- 2 tablespoons unsalted butter
- 6 sprigs fresh thyme

Kosher salt and freshly ground black pepper

for a crowd

As anyone who's served dinner at midnight for a 7 p.m. party knows, the hardest parts of feeding a lot of people at once or hosting an occasion are planning the menu and nailing the timing. The menus in this section combine recipes from throughout the book with some brand-new ones to create the perfect game plan for some of our favorite parties and occasions. Aside from planning your dishes for you, we've broken down the recipes into an actual time line for how to put it all together without abandoning your guests or breaking a sweat—and so that you still get to enjoy the fruits of your labor, too.

date night

SERVES 2

Whether it's your first date, eighth date, or too-many-to-count date, this menu is the way to someone's heart. (We've tested this—it's 100 percent true.) Few gifts say "I'm into you" better than a rib eye and chocolate tart. These dishes are easy enough to accomplish alone, but best taken on with your favorite sous chef.

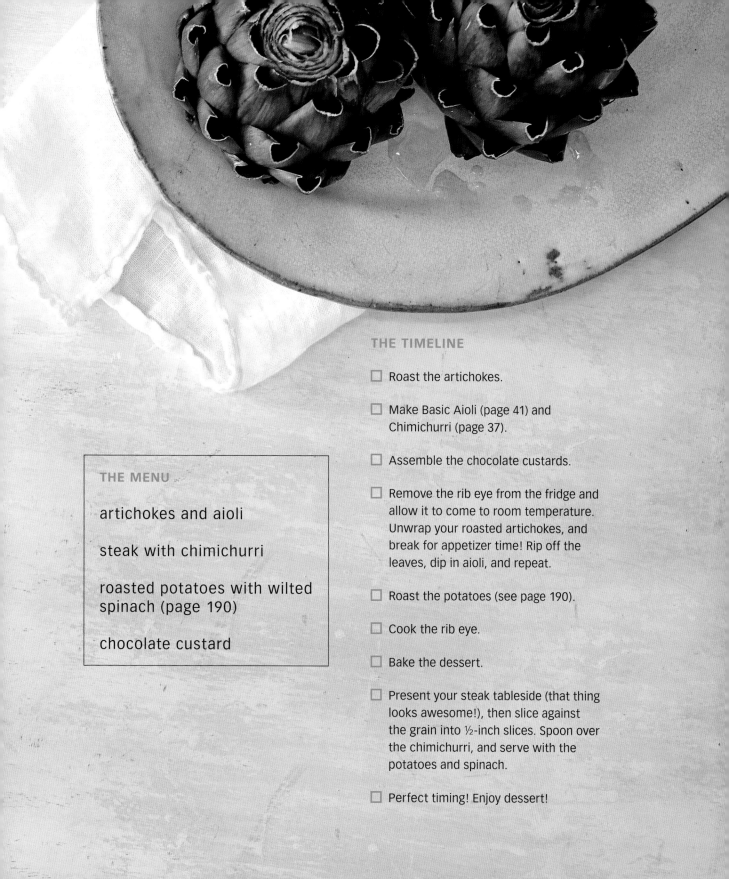

THE MENU

artichokes and aioli

steak with chimichurri

roasted potatoes with wilted spinach (page 190)

chocolate custard

THE TIMELINE

☐ Roast the artichokes.

☐ Make Basic Aioli (page 41) and Chimichurri (page 37).

☐ Assemble the chocolate custards.

☐ Remove the rib eye from the fridge and allow it to come to room temperature. Unwrap your roasted artichokes, and break for appetizer time! Rip off the leaves, dip in aioli, and repeat.

☐ Roast the potatoes (see page 190).

☐ Cook the rib eye.

☐ Bake the dessert.

☐ Present your steak tableside (that thing looks awesome!), then slice against the grain into ½-inch slices. Spoon over the chimichurri, and serve with the potatoes and spinach.

☐ Perfect timing! Enjoy dessert!

artichokes and aioli

3 **cloves garlic**
2 **artichokes**
1 **lemon**
½ **tablespoon extra-virgin**
   olive oil
¼ **cup mayonnaise**
Kosher salt and freshly ground
   black pepper

1. Preheat the oven to 425°F.

2. Peel the garlic and halve 2 of the cloves. Set the third clove aside. Slice off the top thirds of the artichokes and trim the stems so they can sit flat. Place 2 halves of garlic in the center of each artichoke. Halve the lemon and set aside one half. Squeeze the juice of ½ lemon over the artichokes, drizzle with the olive oil, and season with salt and pepper. Wrap in foil and roast until tender, about 1 hour.

3. While the artichokes roast, mince the remaining garlic. In a small bowl, whisk together the minced garlic, mayonnaise, and juice of the remaining ½ lemon. Taste and add salt and pepper as needed. Refrigerate until ready to serve with the artichokes for dipping.

steak with chimichurri

1 tablespoon extra-virgin
   olive oil
1 1-pound bone-in rib eye steak
   (about 1 inch thick)
Chimichurri (page 37)
Kosher salt and freshly ground
   black pepper

In a large ovenproof pan, heat the olive oil over medium-high heat. Pat the steak dry and season on both sides with salt and pepper. When the oil is shimmering, add the steak and sear, without moving, until browned on the outside, flipping halfway through, about 6 minutes. Transfer the pan to the oven (the potatoes will be in there, too) and roast until medium-rare, about 5 minutes. Transfer to a cutting board and allow to rest for 10 minutes before serving and slicing.

chocolate custard

3 large eggs
½ cup heavy cream
5 tablespoons whole milk
2 tablespoons granulated sugar
5 ounces semisweet chocolate
   chips
½ tablespoon powdered sugar

1. Preheat the oven to 325°F.

2. In a large heatproof bowl, beat the eggs and set aside.

3. In a medium pot, combine the cream, milk, and granulated sugar. Bring to a simmer over medium heat, then immediately remove from the heat. Add the chocolate to the cream mixture and stir until melted and smooth, about 1 minute. While whisking, slowly pour the chocolate mixture into the bowl with the eggs, whisking until smooth. Divide the mixture evenly among 4 ramekins and refrigerate until ready to bake.

4. Bake until the custard is set, 35 to 40 minutes. Remove and allow to cool slightly, then sprinkle with the powdered sugar and serve. There's always room for extra dessert. . . .

cocktail party

SERVES 6

Here we present to you our best and most treasured cocktail and no-fuss hors d'oeuvres recipes. These snacks won't leave you stressed before friends arrive, and won't leave guests hungry after they depart. It's up to you to mix and match our suggestions—but fair warning: Consuming *all* these drinks might not have you feeling so hot the next day.

old fashioned with burnt orange

rosemary-thyme vodka lemonade

elderflower gin gimlet

tequila negroni margaritas

spicy roasted nuts

tuna tartare with soy and cucumber

prosciutto-stuffed figs

☐ .Take inventory of your alcohol supply, replenish as needed, and go buy ice.

☐ Chill the glasses as needed.

☐ Prepare your snacks for the evening and taste test them.

☐ Before your guests arrive, quickly tidy up and put on some good music.

☐ Channel your inner Tom Cruise and make some cocktails!

☐ Have a great party; convince one of your guests to make you Weekend Brunch the next morning (page 172).

spicy roasted nuts

4 tablespoons (½ stick)
  unsalted butter
2 fresh red Thai chiles
2 sprigs fresh rosemary
4 sprigs fresh thyme
¾ cup raw almonds
¾ cup raw walnuts
¾ cup raw cashews
½ tablespoon chili powder
1 tablespoon light brown sugar
1 teaspoon flaky sea salt, such
  as Maldon
Kosher salt and freshly ground
  black pepper

1. Preheat the oven to 350°F. Line a baking sheet with parchment paper.

2. Melt the butter. Thinly slice the Thai chiles. Finely chop the rosemary and thyme leaves. While the butter is still warm, pour it into a large bowl and add the herbs, fresh chiles, nuts, chili powder, and brown sugar, stirring to dissolve the sugar. Be sure the nuts are mostly submerged. Allow to soak at room temperature for about 20 minutes.

3. Transfer the mixture to the lined baking sheet and spread it into a single layer, discarding any excess butter. Season the nuts lightly with kosher salt and heavily with black pepper, then toss to combine. Roast until golden and fragrant, about 15 minutes. Remove from the oven and immediately sprinkle with the sea salt. Serve warm or at room temperature.

prosciutto-stuffed figs

1 pint fresh figs, or 1 package
  dried
2 slices prosciutto
1 tablespoon honey
Flaky sea salt, such as Maldon

Slice about three-fourths of the way through the figs. Cut the prosciutto into 1-inch pieces. Loosely fold the prosciutto and stuff into the figs. Pierce with a toothpick. Drizzle with the honey and sprinkle with sea salt before serving.

tuna tartare with soy and cucumber

½ clove garlic
½-inch knob fresh ginger
2 tablespoons soy sauce
1 teaspoon sesame oil
¼ teaspoon wasabi paste
1 pound sushi-grade tuna
1 English cucumber
Kosher salt

1. Finely grate the garlic and ginger on a Microplane. Transfer to a large bowl and whisk in the soy sauce, sesame oil, and wasabi paste.

2. Cut the tuna into ⅛-inch dice. Add to the bowl with the soy mixture and gently fold to mix. Taste and season with salt as needed.

3. Cut the cucumber into ⅛-inch-thick rounds. Spoon the tartare onto cucumber slices and serve.

rosemary-thyme vodka lemonade

¾ **cup sugar**
1 **sprig fresh rosemary**
6 **sprigs fresh thyme, plus**
   more for garnish
2 **cups water**
12 **lemons**
2¼ **cups vodka**
   Ice cubes, for serving

1. In a small pot, combine the sugar, rosemary and thyme sprigs, and water. Bring to a boil and stir until the sugar has dissolved. Remove the pan from the heat and allow the mixture to cool.

2. Juice the lemons into a large pitcher. Add the rosemary-thyme syrup and vodka and stir to combine. Chill until ready to serve.

3. Serve over ice with a sprig of thyme for garnish.

elderflower gin gimlet

½ cup sugar
½ cup water
12 limes
6 tablespoons St-Germain
elderflower liqueur
2 cups gin
1 cup seltzer
Ice cubes, for serving

1. Place 6 highball glasses in the freezer to chill.

2. In a small pot, combine the sugar and water and bring to a boil over medium heat, stirring until the sugar is dissolved. Remove the pot from the heat and allow the mixture to cool.

3. Juice the limes into a large pitcher. Add the sugar syrup, elderflower liqueur, and gin and stir well to combine.

4. Just before serving, add the seltzer and ice to the pitcher and stir quickly to chill. Serve over ice in chilled highball glasses.

tequila negroni margaritas

2 oranges
½ cup kosher salt
6 limes
1 tablespoon Rose's lime juice
6 ounces Campari
2¼ cups blanco tequila
1 cup seltzer
Ice cubes, for serving

1. Place 6 lowball glasses in the freezer to chill.

2. Zest and halve the oranges. On a small plate, combine the salt and orange zest.

3. Halve the limes. Squeeze the oranges and limes (reserve 2 of the juiced limes) into a large pitcher. Add the Rose's lime juice, Campari, tequila, and seltzer. Stir to combine.

4. Rub the rims of the glasses with the reserved limes. Turn upside-down and dip into the orange salt. Add ice cubes to the glasses and pour the margaritas over.

old fashioned with burnt orange

2 oranges
6 brown sugar cubes
6 dashes of Angostura bitters
2¼ cups rye whiskey
3 tablespoons cold water
Ice cubes, for serving

1. Peel off 6 strips of orange zest. Halve the oranges. Place a medium pan over medium heat. When the pan is warm, add the oranges cut-side down. Cook until the flesh is slightly charred, about 3 minutes.

2. Set out 6 lowball glasses. To each, add 1 cube of the sugar and 1 dash bitters and muddle. Divide the rye evenly.

Add ½ tablespoon water, a squeeze of charred orange juice, and 3 ice cubes to each glass. Garnish each with a strip of orange zest.

fancy pants dinner party

SERVES 4 TO 6

Sometimes you just feel fancy. Go with this decadent menu when the mood to take your dinner party game up a notch or two.

THE MENU

seared duck breast

tuna tartare with soy and
cucumber (page 161)

whole roasted carrots
(page 193)

parmesan risotto with
seasonal vegetables
(page 48)

wine-poached pears with
vanilla bean mascarpone
(page 214)

THE TIMELINE

☐ Prepare and poach the pears for
dessert.

☐ Preheat the oven and prepare
the ingredients for your risotto,
carrots, and tartare.

☐ Assemble your tartare and have
a snack (you've earned it!).

☐ Start the risotto.

☐ Roast the duck and the carrots.

☐ Finish your risotto.

☐ Present your work tableside
(man, that's fancy!).

☐ Sit down, pour some wine, and
enjoy your hard work.

☐ Reduce the pear liquid while
your guests clear plates.

☐ Scoop up a perfect bite of
pears and mascarpone and pat
yourself on the back for a job
fancily done.

seared duck breast

> 4 duck breasts
> ½ orange
> ¾ cup dark soy sauce
> 2½ tablespoons honey
>   Kosher salt and freshly ground
>   black pepper

1. Preheat the oven to 400°F.

2. Pat the duck dry. Halve the oranges.

3. Using a sharp knife, score the duck skin in a crisscross pattern, taking care not to cut through to the flesh. Season on both sides with salt and pepper. Place skin-side down in a large ovenproof pan over medium heat. Cook until the fat is rendered and the skin is beginning to crisp, about 15 minutes.

4. Meanwhile, in a large shallow bowl, whisk together the soy sauce, honey, and orange juice. Season with salt and pepper.

5. Remove the duck from the pan and carefully pour off the excess fat, then return the duck to the pan flesh-side down and set over medium heat. Pour the marinade over and cook until the bottom is golden, about 1 minute. Transfer the pan to the oven. Roast until medium-rare, 7 to 9 minutes. Remove the pan from the oven and transfer the duck to a cutting board, reserving the marinade in the pan. Allow to rest for 5 minutes, then thinly slice crosswise. Serve with the reserved marinade spooned over.

sunday supper

SERVES 4 TO 6

Sunday night dinner is one of Elana's favorite traditions.
Without fail, she cooks for her family at the end of every
week, and roast chicken is frequently the star of the menu.
Use our timeline to have a Sunday night feast on the table
without slaving over it all day. Nothing chases off the
"Sunday Scaries" better than a great meal.

THE MENU

roast chicken

roasted apple and fennel
salad with cider vinaigrette
(page 201)

roasted green beans
(page 196)

chocolate brioche bread
pudding (page 209)

THE TIMELINE

☐ Preheat the oven and prepare
your ingredients.

☐ Pop that bird in the oven.

☐ Whisk up your French
vinaigrette.

☐ Assemble your bread pudding
(and be sure to taste test the
chocolate for quality control).

☐ Remove the chicken, let it rest,
and admire it in all its golden
glory.

☐ Roast the vegetables.

☐ Carve the chicken, get the bread
pudding into the oven, and serve
dinner.

☐ Dig into dessert while chasing
away the Sunday Scaries.

roast chicken

1 large chicken (about
   6 pounds)
1½ pounds Yukon Gold or Red
   Bliss potatoes
½ lemon
4 sprigs fresh thyme
2 tablespoons extra-virgin
   olive oil
2 tablespoons French Herb
   Rub (page 27)
Kosher salt and freshly ground
   black pepper

1. Preheat the oven to 450°F.

2. Remove the chicken from the fridge and bring to room temperature, about 30 minutes.

3. Cut the potatoes into ¼-inch slices.

4. Pat the chicken as dry as possible, both inside and out. Generously season the cavity with salt and pepper, then stuff it with the lemon half and thyme sprigs. Place the chicken breast-side up on a cutting board and use kitchen twine to tightly tie the legs together. Rub the outside of the chicken with the olive oil, then season all over with the herb rub and salt and pepper.

5. Arrange the potato slices in an even layer in the bottom of a large ovenproof sauté pan or roasting pan. Season with salt and pepper. Place the chicken on top of the potatoes, or on a roasting rack set over the potatoes if using a roasting pan. Roast on the bottom rack of the oven until the skin is golden, and the juices run clear, about 1 hour 15 minutes.

6. As soon as the chicken has roasted, remove from the pan and set on a cutting board, loosely cover with foil, and allow to rest for about 15 minutes before serving.

7. Cut off and discard the kitchen twine. Using a carving knife or chef's knife, cut between the thigh and the breasts to remove the legs. Cut between the thigh and the drumstick, in between the joint, to separate the legs into 2 pieces. Starting at the breast bone, slice off each breast. Arrange on a platter with the potatoes.

CHEFFY NUGGET: Ask the butcher to remove the wishbone from the chicken to make carving easier.

weekend brunch

SERVES 4 TO 6

Brunch is probably the meal you're most likely to go out for, but having people come to you instead is a surprisingly fun way to start your day—plus, you can stay in your pajamas that much longer. Much of the menu can be prepared a day ahead, so all you have to do is roll out of bed and pop stuff into the oven.

THE MENU

sweet onion, spinach,
and goat cheese frittata
(page 122)

french toast casserole

hash browns

sugar-rubbed bacon

THE TIMELINE

☐ Brew some strong coffee,
preheat the oven, and prepare
the frittata ingredients.

☐ Assemble your French toast
casserole and let the custardy
goodness soak in.

☐ Prepare your hash brown
ingredients and boil the
potatoes. Mmm, hash browns.

☐ Smash the potatoes and cook
the scallions.

☐ Bake the casserole and bacon
(has anything ever smelled
better?).

☐ Brown the potatoes and
caramelize the onion for the
frittata.

☐ Cook the frittata, change out
of pajamas (if you must), and
reheat the hash browns. Garnish
the frittata and serve.

french toast casserole

> 1 loaf challah bread or brioche
>   (about 1 pound)
> 2 cups whole milk
> 1 tablespoon vanilla extract
> 6 large eggs
> Pinch of ground nutmeg
> Kosher salt

1. Preheat the oven to 375°F.

2. Cut the bread into 2-inch pieces. In a medium bowl, whisk together the milk, vanilla, eggs, nutmeg, and a pinch of salt. Assemble the bread in an even layer in a medium square baking dish (about 12 x 12 x 2 inches). Pour over the milk mixture and allow to soak at room temperature for at least 10 minutes, or cover and refrigerate overnight.

3. Transfer the French toast casserole to the oven and bake until set and golden, about 40 minutes.

sugar-rubbed bacon

> 1¼ pounds thick-cut slices slab
>   bacon (about 18 slices)
> 3 tablespoons light brown
>   sugar

1. Preheat the oven to 375°F.

2. Fit a cooling rack into a rimmed baking sheet and arrange the bacon on it in a single layer. Sprinkle evenly with the brown sugar and transfer to the oven. Bake until the bacon is crisping and the sugar is caramelized, about 30 minutes.

hash browns

> 4 large russet potatoes (about
>   4 pounds)
> 4 scallions
> 2 to 3 tablespoons extra-virgin
>   olive oil
> 2 tablespoons unsalted butter
> Kosher salt and freshly ground
>   black pepper

1. Cut the potatoes into 2-inch pieces and place in a medium pot with cold water to cover. Bring to a boil over high heat. Add a generous pinch of salt and cook until just tender, about 8 minutes.

2. Meanwhile, thinly slice the scallions on a diagonal. In a large pan, cast iron if available, heat 1 tablespoon of the olive oil over medium heat until shimmering. Add the scallions and cook until softened, about 5 minutes. Remove to a plate.

3. Drain the potatoes and lay on a large plate or baking sheet to air-dry, 12 to 15 minutes. Once dry, gently smash. Season all over with salt and pepper and set aside.

4. In the pan used to cook the scallions, melt the butter over medium-high heat. When the butter is foamy, add the potatoes and press down on them with a large spatula or small pan. Cook, without moving, until browning on the bottom, about 15 minutes, then remove to a plate.

5. Return the scallions to the pan, add another 1 to 2 table-spoons olive oil, and set over medium-high heat. When the oil is shimmering, return the potatoes, browned-side up, and cook until golden on the second side, continuing to press down, 10 to 15 minutes longer. Remove the pan from the heat and set aside.

6. Just before serving, return the hash browns to medium-high heat and cook until sizzling, 3 to 5 minutes. Taste and add salt and pepper as needed.

backyard barbecue

SERVES 4 TO 6

We feel antsy all year waiting for barbecue season to come around. As soon as summer hits, we start craving burgers, creamy, crunchy slaw, anything slathered with pesto, and warm berry desserts. This lineup is ideal for Memorial Day, Labor Day, and all the days in between. To work ahead, assemble the fruit crumble the day before, then allow it to come to room temperature before baking.

THE MENU

spicy marinated watermelon

pesto orzo with feta

hickory burgers

summer snap pea slaw
(page 199)

seasonal fruit crumble
(page 210)

THE TIMELINE

☐ Prepare and marinate the
watermelon.

☐ Prepare and assemble the
crumble.

☐ Make the slaw, cook the orzo,
and crisp your burger onions.

☐ Dress the orzo in pesto—and
taste some for good measure.

☐ Fire up the grill, preheat the
oven, and cook the burgers.

☐ Throw that crumble in the oven.

☐ Go sit outside and bite into a
juicy burger, creamy slaw, and
crispy onions. Yum!

☐ Dig into the crumble . . . . if you
still have room.

spicy marinated watermelon

2 jalapeños
3 limes
6 cups large diced watermelon
½ bunch fresh mint
Kosher salt

Halve the jalapeños lengthwise, scrape out the seeds, and finely chop. Halve the limes and squeeze the juice into a large bowl. Add the jalapeños and whisk together. Add the watermelon, season lightly with salt, and toss to coat. Cover with plastic wrap and allow to marinate in the fridge for at least 1 hour and up to 3 hours. Tear the mint leaves and sprinkle over the watermelon before serving.

hickory burgers

> 1 yellow onion
> 2 tablespoons extra-virgin olive oil
> 2 pounds (85% lean) ground beef
> 6 tablespoons barbecue sauce
> 1 tablespoon Dijon mustard
> 1 tablespoon canola oil
> 6 hamburger buns
> Ketchup, mustard, and pickles, for serving
> Kosher salt and freshly ground black pepper

1. Halve the onion and thinly slice. In a large pan, heat the olive oil over medium-high heat until shimmering, add the onion, season with salt and pepper, and cook, stirring frequently, until tender and browning in spots, about 8 minutes. Remove from the pan and set aside.

2. In a large bowl, combine the beef, barbecue sauce, and mustard. Season generously with salt and pepper and combine using your hands. Form into 6 equal patties and place on a large plate. Using your thumb, make a dimple in the center of each patty.

3. Preheat a grill to medium-high heat. Brush the grill grates with the canola oil. When the grill is hot, add the burgers and grill until browned on the outside and medium-rare, about 5 minutes per side. (Alternatively, cook, in batches, in a large pan over medium-high heat.) Remove from the heat and allow to rest for about 5 minutes.

4. While the burgers rest, place the buns cut-side down on the grill and cook until toasted, about 2 minutes per side.

5. Top the burgers with the onion, pickles, ketchup, and mustard, as desired.

pesto orzo with feta

> 1 lemon
> ¼ cup pine nuts
> 2 cups orzo
> 1 cup crumbled feta cheese
> ½ cup pesto, store-bought or homemade (page 39)

1. Bring a large pot of water to a boil over high heat for the pasta. Zest the lemon, then halve it. In a medium pan, toast the pine nuts over medium heat until fragrant and golden, about 5 minutes. Remove the nuts to a plate.

2. When the water comes to a boil, add the orzo and a generous pinch of salt and cook until tender, about 8 minutes or according to the package instructions. Drain and transfer to a large serving bowl.

3. Add the pesto, lemon zest, and lemon juice to the orzo. Stir to combine, then gently stir in the feta. Garnish with the pine nuts. Stir just before serving to remove any clumps.

thanksgiving dinner

SERVES 6 TO 8

This menu is a mash-up of our absolute favorite Thanksgiving recipes (and we take Thanksgiving cooking really seriously). Few cooking adventures can be more daunting than Turkey Day—high expectations, out-of-towners, and the prospect of roasting a giant, whole bird. But with some planning and organization, you'll find it's not so bad after all.

THE turkey with citrus herb butter and apricot glaze

cognac gravy

mushroom, sausage, and sage stuffing

crispy brussels sprouts
(page 192)

spiced mashed sweet potatoes

epic pecan and pumpkin pie
(page 220)

THE TIMELINE

The Day Before:

☐ Mentally prepare yourself; it's going to be a big two days.

☐ Prepare your compound butter and your ingredients for the stuffing and sides.

☐ Cook and assemble your stuffing.

☐ Prepare and bake the pie.

Thanksgiving Day:

☐ Pour a stiff drink. Your in-laws are on their way.

☐ Prepare and roast the turkey.

☐ Bake the stuffing; when the top is crunchy (but not before!), steal a taste.

☐ Make the glaze and be thankful you're not sitting in traffic today.

☐ Roast the vegetables while the turkey finishes roasting.

☐ Glaze the turkey.

☐ Make the Cognac gravy (a swig for the chef!) and rest the turkey.

☐ You made it! Happy Thanksgiving!

THE turkey with citrus herb butter and apricot glaze

3   oranges
4   sprigs fresh rosemary
10 sprigs fresh sage
10 sprigs fresh thyme
8   tablespoons (1 stick)
    unsalted butter, at room
    temperature
1   12-pound turkey
4   onions
1   head garlic
6   carrots
2   tablespoons extra-virgin
    olive oil
1   cup apricot jam
¼   cup soy sauce
¼   cup white wine
1   tablespoon maple syrup
Kosher salt and freshly ground
    black pepper

1. Zest the oranges. Finely chop half the rosemary, sage, and thyme leaves. In a medium bowl, combine the butter, orange zest, and chopped rosemary, sage, and thyme. Season with salt and pepper. Place the mixture on a piece of plastic wrap and roll into a log, twisting the ends to seal tightly. Chill in the fridge for at least 1 hour.

2. On Thanksgiving day, preheat the oven to 425°F.

3. Remove the turkey from the fridge to come to room temperature. Halve the oranges. Halve 1 onion and roughly chop the rest. Halve the garlic head horizontally. Roughly chop the carrots. Season the turkey cavity with salt and pepper and stuff with the halved onion, garlic, ½ orange, and remaining whole herb sprigs. Rub the herbed butter mixture over the flesh and under the skin, pulling the skin back into place. Rub the skin with ½ orange, then with 2 tablespoons olive oil. Season the skin generously with salt and pepper.

4. Scatter the roughly chopped onions and carrots on the bottom of a roasting pan. Pour in 3½ cups water. Place the turkey breast-side down on a roasting rack and roast for 1 hour 45 minutes, basting occasionally.

5. While the turkey roasts, squeeze the orange juice from the remaining 2½ oranges into a small pot. Add the apricot jam, soy sauce, white wine, maple syrup, and 1½ cups water. Bring to a boil over medium heat and cook to reduce by one-third, 15 to 17 minutes. Remove the apricot glaze from the heat and set aside.

6. Remove the turkey from the oven and flip breast-side up. Reduce the oven temperature to 400°F and return the turkey to the oven for 25 minutes longer, basting occasionally.

7. Remove the turkey again and brush the apricot glaze over the skin. Return to the oven once more and roast until the skin is crisp and browned and the turkey is cooked through and the juices run clear when you cut between the leg and the thigh, 25 to 30 minutes. If you're unsure, insert an instant-read thermometer into the thickest part of the thigh; it should read 165°F. Watch the turkey closely at this point; if the skin begins to burn, cover with foil for the remainder of the cooking time.

8. Remove the turkey from the oven and cover with foil. Set aside to rest for at least 20 minutes before carving. Remove the legs and cut between the thigh and the drumstick at the joint. Remove the thigh bone and shred into large pieces. Carve the breasts off the bone and thinly slice crosswise.

on the side

Often meant to be punctuation to a main course, side dishes can sometimes steal the whole show. They're often our favorite part of the meal (though that might just be because of our extreme love of potatoes). Here are some basic sides that are versatile enough to work with just about any type of meal, plus a few variations to keep things interesting on your dinner table.

spiced mashed sweet potatoes

3 pounds sweet potatoes
3 tablespoons extra-virgin
  olive oil
1 teaspoon ground coriander
1 teaspoon ground cumin
¼ teaspoon ground cloves
2 tablespoons maple syrup
Kosher salt and freshly ground
  black pepper

1. Preheat the oven to 425°F.

2. Cut the sweet potatoes into large dice. On a baking sheet, toss with the olive oil, coriander, cumin, cloves, and maple syrup. Season with salt and pepper and arrange in a single layer. Roast until tender, 15 to 20 minutes. Mash using a large fork or potato masher until mostly smooth.

cognac gravy

2 cups chicken stock
3 shallots
8 tablespoons (1 stick)
  unsalted butter
¼ cup all-purpose flour
1 tablespoon Cognac
Kosher salt and freshly ground
  black pepper

1. In a small saucepan, bring the chicken stock to a simmer over medium heat.

2. Mince the shallots. In a medium saucepan, melt the butter over medium heat. When the butter is foamy, add the shallots and cook until softened, about 5 minutes. Sprinkle with the flour and whisk until the mixture is golden brown and smooth. Add the Cognac and cook for 30 seconds. Add the warm chicken stock and stir to combine. Cook until the mixture is thickened, 5 to 7 minutes. Taste and add salt and pepper as needed.

on the side

Often meant to be punctuation to a main course, side dishes can sometimes steal
the whole show. They're often our favorite part of the meal (though that might just
be because of our extreme love of potatoes). Here are some basic sides that are
versatile enough to work with just about any type of meal, plus a few variations to
keep things interesting on your dinner table.

mushroom, sausage, and sage stuffing

1½	pounds cremini mushrooms
2	onions
4	stalks celery
2	sprigs fresh sage
4	sprigs fresh thyme
1	large ciabatta or sourdough loaf
¾	pound sweet Italian sausage
2	tablespoons extra-virgin olive oil
2	tablespoons unsalted butter
2	cups chicken stock
2	large eggs
	Kosher salt and freshly ground black pepper

1. Preheat the oven to 350°F.

2. Quarter the mushrooms. Finely dice the onions. Finely chop the celery. Finely chop the sage leaves. Strip the thyme leaves from the stems. Cut the bread into large dice to yield about 8 cups and arrange on 2 baking sheets in a single layer. Toast in the oven until crunchy, about 15 minutes.

3. While the croutons toast, remove and discard the casings from the sausage. In a large pan, heat 1 tablespoon of the olive oil over medium-high heat until shimmering. Add the sausage and break it up with a wooden spoon as it browns, 8 to 10 minutes. Remove to a large ovenproof baking dish.

4. Place the same pan over medium heat and add the mushrooms, sage, and thyme. Cook until the mushrooms are golden brown, 7 to 9 minutes. Transfer the mushrooms to the baking dish with the sausage.

5. Add 1 tablespoon of the butter and the remaining 1 tablespoon olive oil to the pan and heat over medium heat. When the butter is foamy, add the onions and celery and sauté until soft and translucent, 5 to 7 minutes. Transfer to the baking dish.

6. Add the croutons to the baking dish along with the chicken stock and eggs. Season with salt and pepper and stir to combine. Spread in an even layer and dot with the remaining 1 tablespoon butter. (If making ahead, cover with foil and refrigerate overnight.) Cover with foil and bake for 20 minutes. Uncover and continue to bake until crisp on top, about 20 minutes longer.

perfect roasted potatoes

SERVES 2 TO 4

> 1 pound mini creamer or
>   fingerling potatoes
> 2 sprigs fresh rosemary
> 2 tablespoons extra-virgin
>   olive oil
> Kosher salt and freshly ground
>   black pepper

1. Preheat the oven to 425°F.

2. Halve the potatoes. Finely chop the rosemary leaves.

3. On a baking sheet, toss the potatoes with the rosemary, olive oil, salt, and pepper. Arrange cut-side down in a single layer, being sure to space apart. If necessary, use 2 baking sheets or work in batches—space is the key to crispy potatoes!

4. Roast until the cut sides are golden brown and the potatoes are tender, 18 to 20 minutes. Season with salt and serve hot.

VARIATIONS

Roasted Potatoes with Wilted Spinach: For extra color and nutrients, toss the hot potatoes right out of the oven with 3 cups baby spinach just until wilted. Add 1 more tablespoon olive oil if needed.

Parmesan-Crusted Potatoes: After halving the potatoes, spread the cut sides with 2 tablespoons Dijon mustard and sprinkle with ¼ cup grated Parmesan cheese. Before putting the potatoes on the baking sheet, drizzle the baking sheet with ½ tablespoon extra-virgin olive oil. Instead of tossing the potatoes, arrange them cut-side down in a single layer. Sprinkle with the rosemary and salt and pepper. Drizzle with 3 tablespoons olive oil. Roast as directed.

creamy french-style mashed potatoes

SERVES 2 TO 4

> 3 pounds Yukon Gold
>   potatoes
> 1½ cups whole milk
> 8 tablespoons (1 stick)
>   unsalted butter
> Kosher salt and freshly ground
>   black pepper

1. Peel the potatoes and cut into 1-inch pieces. Place in a large pot with cold water to cover and bring to a boil over high heat. When the water comes to a boil, add a generous pinch of salt and boil until the potatoes are tender, about 12 minutes. Drain the potatoes, then pass through a ricer or food mill.

2. In a medium sauté pan, heat the milk and butter over medium heat. Simmer until the butter is melted and the milk is warm. Reduce to the lowest possible heat. Add the potatoes and stir to combine. Taste and add salt and pepper as needed.

twice-baked potatoes

SERVES 4

> 4   1-pound russet potatoes
> ½ cup whole milk, at room
>   temperature
> 6   tablespoons unsalted butter,
>   at room temperature
>   Kosher salt and freshly ground
>   black pepper

1. Preheat the oven to 425°F.

2. Pierce the potatoes all over with a fork and microwave until tender, 8 to 12 minutes, turning halfway through.

3. Halve the potatoes lengthwise and use a small spoon to carefully scoop out the flesh into a medium bowl, leaving a thin border of flesh in the potato skins. Add the milk and butter to the bowl and mash until smooth. Season with salt and pepper.

4. Refill the potato skins evenly with the mashed potatoes and arrange in a single layer on a baking sheet. Bake until warmed through, 10 to 12 minutes.

VARIATIONS

Spanakopita-Style Twice-Baked Potatoes: Add 4 ounces crumbled feta and 4 cups sautéed baby spinach to the bowl with the potato flesh, milk, and butter. Mix until combined and bake as directed.

Wasabi Twice-Baked Potatoes: Add 2 thinly sliced scallions and 1 tablespoon wasabi paste to the bowl with the potato flesh, milk, and butter. Mix until combined and bake as directed. Garnish with 3 tablespoons toasted sesame seeds.

crispy brussels sprouts

SERVES 2 TO 4

> 1 pound Brussels sprouts
> 1½ tablespoons extra-virgin
>   olive oil
>   Kosher salt and freshly ground
>   black pepper

1. Preheat the oven to 425°F.

2. Halve the Brussels sprouts through the root. On a baking sheet, toss the Brussels sprouts with the olive oil and salt and pepper. Arrange cut-side down in a single layer. Roast until tender, 20 to 25 minutes.

VARIATIONS

Sweet and Crunchy Brussels Sprouts: Roast the Brussels sprouts as directed for 18 to 20 minutes, then remove from the oven, drizzle with 2 tablespoons maple syrup, and scatter 2 tablespoons roughly chopped hazelnuts on top. Stir to combine. Return to the oven and roast until the Brussels sprouts are deep golden brown and crisp and the hazelnuts are beginning to brown, about 5 minutes longer.

Pancetta Brussels Sprouts: Cut 2 ounces pancetta into ¼-inch dice. Toss the pancetta with the Brussels sprouts and roast as directed.

whole roasted carrots

> 1 pound carrots (about ¾ inch
> diameter), with tops
> 1½ tablespoons extra-virgin
> olive oil
> 4 sprigs fresh mint
> 1 lemon
> Kosher salt and freshly ground
> black pepper

1. Preheat the oven to 425°F.

2. Trim off most of the green leafy tops from the carrots, leaving 1 inch of stem.

3. On a baking sheet, toss the carrots with the olive oil and salt and pepper. Arrange in a single layer, spacing apart, and roast until just tender, 18 to 20 minutes.

4. While the carrots roast, roughly tear the mint leaves. Halve the lemon.

5. As soon as the carrots come out of the oven, immediately toss with the mint and the lemon juice. Serve warm or at room temperature.

CHEFFY NUGGET: To test for perfect carrot doneness—still with some bite but not mushy—slide a small knife into the thick end of one; if the knife meets little resistance, they're ready to munch.

winter greens gratin

SERVES 4

¾ pound Swiss chard
½ pound curly kale
4 cloves garlic
1 small yellow onion
2 tablespoons extra-virgin
   olive oil
½ lemon
6 cups baby spinach
½ cup whole milk
¼ cup heavy cream
1 cup shredded Gruyère cheese
2 tablespoons panko bread
   crumbs
1 tablespoon grated Parmesan
   cheese
Kosher salt and freshly ground
   black pepper

1. Preheat the oven to 400°F.

2. Cut the Swiss chard stems and leaves crosswise into ½-inch slices, keeping them separate. Cut the kale leaves crosswise into ½-inch slices, discarding the stems. Mince the garlic. Finely dice the onion.

3. In an 8-inch ovenproof sauté pan, heat the olive oil over medium heat until shimmering. Add the onion and cook until soft and translucent, about 5 minutes. Add the garlic and cook until fragrant, about 1 minute. Add the Swiss chard stems and cook until softening, about 5 minutes. Add the Swiss chard and kale leaves, working in batches if needed, and cook until wilted and softening, about 3 minutes. Squeeze in the lemon juice and stir to combine.

4. Add the spinach and cook until wilted, about 2 minutes. Add the milk and cream and stir to warm through, about 1 minute longer. Remove the pan from the heat. Stir in the Gruyère, then taste and season with salt and pepper as needed. Sprinkle the panko and Parmesan evenly over the top.

5. Cover the gratin with foil and transfer to the oven. Bake until beginning to bubble on the sides, about 10 minutes. Uncover and bake until the bread crumbs are golden, about 10 minutes longer.

roasted green beans

SERVES 2 TO 4

> ¾ **pound green beans**
> 3 **tablespoons walnuts**
> 1½ **tablespoons extra-virgin olive oil**
> **Kosher salt and freshly ground black pepper**

1. Preheat the oven to 425°F.

2. Trim the ends off the green beans. Roughly chop the walnuts.

3. On a baking sheet, toss the green beans with the olive oil and salt and pepper. Arrange in a single layer and roast until bright green, about 10 minutes. Remove the baking sheet from the oven and shake the pan. Scatter over the walnuts and return to the oven until the green beans are browning in spots and the walnuts are toasted and fragrant, about 5 minutes longer. Serve warm or at room temperature.

crispy roasted chickpeas

SERVES 2 TO 4

> 1 **15-ounce can chickpeas**
> 2 **tablespoons extra-virgin olive oil**
> ¼ **teaspoon sweet paprika**
> ⅛ **teaspoon cayenne pepper**
> **Kosher salt and freshly ground black pepper**

1. Preheat the oven to 450°F.

2. Drain and rinse the chickpeas. Pat as dry as possible.

3. On a baking sheet, toss the chickpeas with the olive oil, paprika, cayenne, salt, and black pepper. Arrange in a single layer and roast until crisp, 20 to 25 minutes. Serve warm or at room temperature.

CHEFFY NUGGET: For the crunchiest possible results, arrange the rinsed and dried chickpeas in a single layer on a baking sheet or cutting board. Using a paper towel or kitchen towel, gently rub your hands back and forth over the chickpeas, applying just a little pressure. This way you'll remove the chickpea skins—discard them. Keep in mind that this may shorten your cook time.

17-minute rice

SERVES 2 TO 4

> 1 teaspoon extra-virgin olive
>   oil
> ¾ cup long-grain white rice
> 1½ cups water or chicken or
>   vegetable stock
> Kosher salt

1. Preheat the oven to 375°F.

2. In a medium ovenproof sauté pan, heat the olive oil over medium heat until shimmering. Add the rice and stir to coat. Cook until translucent, 1 to 2 minutes.

3. Add the water or stock and a pinch of salt and increase the heat to high. Bring to a boil, then cover and transfer to the oven. Bake for exactly 17 minutes, without touching the lid. Remove from the oven, uncover, and fluff with a fork. Taste and add salt as needed.

VARIATIONS

Miso-Ginger Rice: When sautéing the rice, add 1 teaspoon minced fresh ginger and 1 tablespoon white miso paste. Cook as directed.

Coconut Rice: Swap out ½ cup water or stock for ½ cup coconut milk and cook as directed.

Spiced Rice: Add 1½ teaspoons of your favorite spice blend to the oil before adding the rice. Cook as directed.

quinoa tabbouleh

SERVES 2 TO 4

> 1 cup quinoa
> 2 cups vegetable stock or
>   water
> 1 beefsteak tomato
> ½ English cucumber
> 1 clove garlic
> ½ red onion
> ¼ cup fresh flat-leaf parsley
>   leaves
> 1 lemon
> 2 tablespoons extra-virgin
>   olive oil
> Kosher salt and freshly ground
>   black pepper

1. In a medium saucepan, combine the quinoa, stock, and a pinch of salt and bring to a boil over high heat. Reduce the heat to low and simmer until the liquid is evaporated and the quinoa is tender, about 15 minutes. Remove the pot from the heat, cover, and allow to stand for about 5 minutes. Uncover and fluff with a fork.

2. While the quinoa cooks, cut the tomato and cucumber into ¼-inch dice. Mince the garlic and onion. Roughly chop the parsley leaves. Halve the lemon.

3. In a large bowl, whisk together the garlic, lemon juice, and olive oil. Taste and add salt and pepper as needed. Add the quinoa, tomato, cucumber, garlic, onion, and parsley to the bowl and stir to combine. Taste and add more salt and pepper as needed.

bulgur with almonds

SERVES 2 TO 4

> 1 cup bulgur
> 1 lemon
> 1½ tablespoons extra-virgin
>   olive oil
> ½ teaspoon honey
> ¼ cup sliced almonds
> Kosher salt and freshly ground
>   black pepper

1. Bring a medium pot of water to a boil over high heat.

2. Halve the lemon. Whisk together the lemon juice, olive oil, and honey. Taste and add salt and pepper as needed.

3. When the water is boiling, add the bulgur and a generous pinch of salt. Cook until tender, about 10 minutes. Drain the bulgur and return it to the pot to allow any excess moisture to evaporate and to cool slightly.

4. Transfer the bulgur and almonds to a large bowl and pour the dressing over. Stir to combine. Taste and add salt and pepper as needed.

apple cider farro with herbs

SERVES 2 TO 4

> 1 cup farro
> 1¼ cups apple cider
> 1 cup water
> 1 bay leaf
> ¼ cup fresh flat-leaf parsley
>   leaves
> ¼ cup fresh mint leaves
> 1 lemon
> 1 tablespoon extra-virgin
>   olive oil
> Kosher salt and freshly ground
>   black pepper

1. In a small saucepan, combine the apple cider, water, bay leaf, and a generous pinch of salt. Bring to a boil over high heat. Add the farro and reduce the heat to medium. Simmer until the farro is tender and the liquid has been absorbed, about 20 minutes.

2. While the farro simmers, pick the parsley and mint leaves, discarding the stems. Zest the lemon, then halve it.

3. When the farro is tender, remove from the heat and discard the bay leaf. Add the lemon juice and olive oil and stir to combine. Allow to cool for about 5 minutes. Stir in the parsley and mint. Taste and add salt and pepper as needed.

summer snap pea slaw

SERVES 2 TO 4

- 1 cup sugar snap peas
- ½ teaspoon Dijon mustard
- 1½ tablespoons whole-grain mustard
- ¼ cup mayonnaise
- 2 tablespoons Greek yogurt
- ½ tablespoon apple cider vinegar
- ½ teaspoon celery seed
- 1 cup shredded green cabbage
- 1 cup shredded red cabbage
- 1 cup shredded carrot
- Kosher salt and freshly ground black pepper

Thinly slice the sugar snap peas crosswise on a diagonal. In a large bowl, whisk together the mustards, mayonnaise, yogurt, vinegar, and celery seed. Add the snap peas, cabbages, and carrot and stir to coat. Taste the slaw and add salt and pepper as needed.

roasted apple and fennel salad with cider vinaigrette

SERVES 2 TO 4

- 1 small bulb fennel
- 1 Gala or Honeycrisp apple, unpeeled
- 3 sprigs fresh tarragon
- 4 sprigs fresh flat-leaf parsley
- 3½ tablespoons extra-virgin olive oil
- 1 tablespoon apple cider vinegar
- 1½ teaspoons Dijon mustard
- 3 cups arugula
- Kosher salt and freshly ground black pepper

1. Preheat the oven to 425°F.

2. Trim off the fennel stalks. Halve the bulb and cut out the tough core. Cut into ¼-inch-thick slices. Cut the apple into ¼-inch-thick slices. Roughly chop the tarragon leaves. Pick the parsley leaves off the stems.

3. On a baking sheet, toss the fennel and apple with 2 tablespoons of the olive oil and salt and pepper. Arrange in a single layer and roast until tender, about 15 minutes.

4. While the fennel and apple roast, in a large bowl, whisk together the vinegar and mustard. While whisking, pour in the remaining 1½ tablespoons olive oil until combined. Taste the dressing and add salt and pepper as needed.

5. Add the arugula, parsley, tarragon, and roasted apple and fennel to the dressing and toss to coat. Taste the salad and season with more salt and pepper as needed.

escarole salad with marcona almonds and crumbled cheese

SERVES 2 TO 4

- 1 small shallot
- 2 tablespoons Marcona almonds
- 1 small head escarole
- 1 tablespoon red wine vinegar
- 1 teaspoon honey
- 1½ tablespoons extra-virgin olive oil
- ¼ cup crumbled Caccio or pecorino cheese
- Kosher salt and freshly ground black pepper

1. Mince the shallot. Roughly chop the almonds. Trim the escarole and tear the leaves into 2-inch pieces.

2. In a large bowl, whisk together the shallot, vinegar, and honey. While whisking, slowly drizzle in the olive oil until emulsified. Taste and season with salt and pepper.

3. Add the escarole and almonds to the dressing and toss to coat. Add the cheese and gently toss using your hands.

corn salad with red onion and basil

SERVES 2 TO 4

3 ears corn
½ small red onion
1 cup mixed cherry tomatoes
1 tablespoon unsalted butter
4 sprigs fresh basil
6 fresh chives
½ tablespoon extra-virgin olive oil
1 tablespoon grated Parmesan cheese
Kosher salt and freshly ground black pepper

1. Shuck the corn and slice the kernels off the cobs into a medium bowl. Finely dice the onion. Halve the tomatoes.

2. In a large pan, melt the butter over medium heat. When the butter is foamy, add the onion and cook until softened, about 5 minutes. Add the corn, increase the heat to medium-high, and cook until warmed through and browning in spots, about 5 minutes longer. Taste and add salt and pepper as needed.

3. While the onion and corn cook, roughly tear the basil leaves. Thinly slice the chives. In a medium serving bowl, toss the cherry tomatoes with the olive oil and salt and pepper.

4. Add the corn to the cherry tomatoes. Stir in the herbs and Parmesan. Serve warm or at room temperature.

marinated kale caesar salad
with croutons and parmesan

SERVES 2 TO 4

1 bunch curly kale
1 small ciabatta roll
1 lemon
2 cloves garlic
2 tablespoons mayonnaise
½ teaspoon anchovy paste
2 tablespoons grated Parmesan cheese
1 tablespoon extra-virgin olive oil
2 ounces whole-block Parmesan cheese
Kosher salt and freshly ground black pepper

1. Discard the kale stems and ribs, then cut the leaves crosswise into ¼-inch slices. Cut the ciabatta into large dice. Halve the lemon. Make a garlic paste (see Cheffy Nugget on page 33).

2. In a large bowl, whisk together the garlic paste, lemon juice, mayonnaise, anchovy paste, and grated Parmesan. Taste the dressing and add salt and pepper as needed. Add the kale and toss to coat. Set aside to marinate for at least 10 minutes or up to 4 hours in the fridge.

3. In a medium pan, heat the olive oil over medium heat until shimmering. Add the bread cubes and season with salt and pepper. Cook until golden brown, about 2 minutes per side.

4. Just before serving, add the croutons to the kale and toss to combine. Transfer to a serving bowl and shave or peel strips of Parmesan over the salad.

CHEFFY NUGGET: Friends don't let friends eat unmarinated kale salads. The tough kale leaves become tender once they've sat in dressing for a few hours, making them much easier to love (and digest). Try this trick with other dressings or even just olive oil and salt.

at the end

We know firsthand that people who love dessert don't always love to bake. But that doesn't mean they can't have their cake and eat it, too! After all, what's a meal without something for your sweet tooth afterward? We've kept all types of dessert-lovers in mind with the recipes in this chapter, ranging from the drop-dead simple to the slightly more elaborate.

coffee granita

Granita, or as we like to call it, "an adult slushie," takes a little bit of time, but requires no technique (aside from properly closing the freezer). You can flavor these however you want—fruit juice and rum are another favorite combination—but we chose coffee because it's how we (and probably lots of you!) like to end a meal.

1. In a 9 x 13-inch baking dish, combine the coffee, ½ cup of the sugar, and the Kahlúa. The mixture should be about ¼ inch deep in the dish. Allow the mixture to cool to room temperature, about 15 minutes.

2. Transfer to the freezer until chilled, about 30 minutes. Remove and scrape the mixture with a fork, until some shavings have come loose. Return to the freezer and continue to scrape every 30 minutes until slushy, about 3 hours.

3. Before serving, in a large bowl, combine the heavy cream and remaining 1½ tablespoons sugar. Using an electric mixer or a whisk, beat until stiff peaks form.

4. Serve the granita with a dollop of whipped cream on top.

CHEFFY NUGGET: The granita is best if eaten the day you make it; otherwise it will freeze into a solid and be difficult to eat.

SERVES 4 TO 6

> 2 **cups hot coffee or espresso (or a combination)**
> ½ **cup plus 1½ tablespoons sugar**
> 1 **tablespoon Kahlúa**
> ½ **cup heavy cream**

chocolate brioche bread pudding

Suzanne learned from her mom early on that there are few better uses for leftover bread than bread pudding—and this one is pure gooey, crunchy comfort food. Once you get this recipe down, experiment with mixing in some more ingredients to make it your own. Cooked fruit, toasted nuts, rum, and warm spices like cardamom are some of our favorite add-ins.

1. Preheat the oven to 350°F. Grease a medium baking dish with butter and set aside.

2. Cut the brioche into large dice. In a large heatproof bowl, whisk together the eggs and vanilla. In a medium pot, combine the milk, sugar, cinnamon, and nutmeg. Bring to a simmer over medium heat, stirring to dissolve the sugar. When small bubbles appear on the surface, remove from the heat. Add the chocolate and stir until melted and smooth.

3. While whisking, slowly pour the milk mixture into the egg mixture until smooth.

4. Arrange the brioche cubes in an even layer in the prepared baking dish, then pour the custard over them. The bread should be two-thirds submerged. Set aside to soak for 10 to 20 minutes.

5. Bake the bread pudding until golden on top and the custard is set, 35 to 40 minutes. Remove from the oven and allow to cool for 5 minutes. Serve warm or at room temperature.

SERVES 4 TO 6

About ½ tablespoon unsalted butter, for greasing the baking dish
4 large eggs
1 teaspoon vanilla extract
2½ cups whole milk
½ cup sugar
½ teaspoon ground cinnamon
⅛ teaspoon ground nutmeg
½ cup semisweet chocolate chips
8 brioche rolls

seasonal fruit crumble

Sorry, pie, crumble is our favorite way to eat fruit for dessert. Gooey, crunchy, and absolutely versatile for any season, this straightforward classic highlights its star ingredients while enhancing them ever so slightly with that sweet crunch on top.

1. Preheat the oven to 350°F.

2. In a large bowl, mix together the seasonal ingredients, ½ cup of the granulated sugar, and 2 squeezes of lemon juice.

3. In a medium bowl, mix together the flour, oats, brown sugar, remaining 1 tablespoon granulated sugar, and a pinch of kosher salt. Cut the butter into 1-inch pieces and add to the bowl. Mix by hand until there is no loose flour or sugar left.

4. Spoon the seasonal fruit mixture into a 9 x 9-inch baking dish. Sprinkle the crumble over the topping. Place the dish on a baking sheet and transfer to the oven.

5. For the summer crumble, bake until the fruit is bubbling and the topping is golden, about 25 minutes.

6. For the fall crumble, cover with foil and bake for 10 minutes, then uncover and continue baking until the fruit is bubbling and the topping is golden, about 25 minutes.

SERVES 4 TO 6

Seasonal ingredients
  (see Seasonal Swaps, below)
½ cup plus 1 tablespoon
  granulated sugar
1 lemon, halved
¾ cup all-purpose flour
½ cup rolled oats
2 tablespoons light brown
  sugar
8 tablespoons (1 stick) cold
  unsalted butter
Kosher salt

SUMMER

1 cup blueberries
1 cup raspberries
1 cup strawberries, cut into
  ½-inch pieces
2 peaches, cut into ½-inch
  pieces
1½ tablespoons cornstarch

FALL

1 pound Honeycrisp or Pink
  Lady apples, peeled, cored,
  and cut into ½-inch pieces
1 pound Bosc pears, peeled,
  cored, and cut into ½-inch
  pieces
1 teaspoon ground cinnamon
1 tablespoon cornstarch

chocolate custard pie

This is a decadent dessert that's easy to pull off for even the most reluctant bakers. With only a small handful of ingredients, this custard is deeply chocolaty, fluffy, and, if we may, quite good at the breakfast table.

1. Preheat the oven to 325°F.

2. In a large heatproof bowl, beat the eggs and set aside.

3. In a medium pot, combine the cream, milk, and granulated sugar. Bring to a simmer over medium heat, 7 to 8 minutes. When small bubbles form on the surface, immediately remove the pot from the heat. Add the chocolate and stir until melted and smooth, about 1 minute.

4. While whisking, slowly add the milk mixture to the eggs, and continue to whisk until smooth. Pour the custard into the pie shell and place on a baking sheet. Bake until just set and very puffed, 45 to 50 minutes.

5. Remove from the oven and let cool for about 30 minutes (the pie will look somewhat sunken) or refrigerate overnight. Serve warm or chilled, garnished with the powdered sugar.

SERVES 8

6 large eggs
1 cup heavy cream
½ cup plus 2 tablespoons whole milk
¼ cup granulated sugar
10 ounces semisweet chocolate chips
1 store-bought 9-inch pie shell
2 tablespoons powdered sugar

CHEFFY NUGGET: Eggs help hold the custard together and give it a silky texture, but be sure to add the hot milk very slowly to avoid scrambling them in the bowl.

wine-poached pears

WITH VANILLA BEAN MASCARPONE

This stunningly beautiful end to a meal is deceptively easy. The pears become tender and turn a vibrant red in a tart-sweet braise of red wine and lemon, offset perfectly by a dollop of tangy-sweet mascarpone.

1. Zest the lemon, then halve it. Peel the pears, halve them lengthwise, core, and cut each into 6 wedges.

2. In a medium saucepan, combine the wine, ½ cup of the sugar, the honey, lemon zest, and 2 squeezes of lemon juice. Bring to a simmer over medium-high heat, stirring to dissolve the sugar. Simmer until the flavors are melded, about 5 minutes. Add the pears, submerging them at least halfway. Cover and poach until tender, 10 to 15 minutes, stirring every 5 minutes.

3. Meanwhile, in a small bowl, stir together the mascarpone, vanilla bean paste, and remaining 1 teaspoon sugar. Set aside in the fridge to chill until ready to serve.

4. Lift the pears from the pot, reserving the poaching liquid in the pot, and divide the pears evenly among bowls. Increase the heat under the pot to high and simmer the poaching liquid until reduced by half and slightly thickened, 6 to 8 minutes.

5. Spoon the liquid over the pears and garnish each bowl with a dollop of vanilla bean mascarpone. Serve warm or at room temperature.

If you're not eating them right away, the pears can be refrigerated with the poaching liquid in an airtight container in the fridge for up to 3 days.

SERVES 4 TO 6

1 lemon
4 Bosc pears
2 cups red wine
½ cup plus 1 teaspoon sugar
¼ cup honey
⅓ cup mascarpone cheese
1 teaspoon vanilla bean paste

CHEFFY NUGGET: Use a melon baller for the easiest and more picture-perfect method of scooping out the pear cores.

greek yogurt and macerated berry panna cotta

Using Greek yogurt in panna cotta gives it a tangy, refreshing flavor while also making it a bit lighter than the traditional version. Take advantage of fresh berries at their peak in the summer to create a swirl that runs through this silky, smooth, and chilled dessert on a hot day. Instead of a large baking dish, you can divide among smaller ramekins or baking dishes, keeping in mind the chilling time will be shorter for smaller vessels.

1. Measure 1 tablespoon water into a small bowl and sprinkle the gelatin on top. Set aside to bloom for about 5 minutes.

2. Meanwhile, halve the lemons and squeeze the juice into a blender or food processor. Add the berries and ¼ cup of the sugar and process until very smooth (see Cheffy Nugget).

3. In a large bowl, combine the yogurt, milk, maple syrup, and remaining ¼ cup plus 2 tablespoons sugar. Add the vanilla bean paste (or if using a vanilla bean, split the pod and scrape the seeds into the bowl) and whisk until smooth.

4. Transfer ½ cup of the yogurt mixture to a small pot and cook over medium-low heat, stirring, just to warm through, about 2 minutes. Add the gelatin mixture and stir until completely dissolved and no longer gritty, about 1 minute longer. Remove from the heat and set aside to cool for 5 to 10 minutes. Then stir the mixture back into the large bowl with the rest of the yogurt mixture until evenly combined.

5. In a large bowl, using an electric mixer or a whisk, whip the heavy cream until stiff peaks form, 2 to 3 minutes. Fold the yogurt mixture into the whipped cream using a large spatula, 1 cup at a time, incorporating each addition completely before adding the next.

6. Pour the panna cotta into an 11 x 7-inch baking dish. Gently pour the berry sauce in a straight line down the middle. Using a fork or a small spoon, swirl the sauce into the panna cotta to create a marbled effect. Gently wrap with plastic and refrigerate until set and no longer wiggly, 8 hours or overnight. Serve chilled.

SERVES 6 TO 8

- 1½ teaspoons unflavored powdered gelatin
- 2 lemons
- 2 cups mixed berries
- ½ cup plus 2 tablespoons sugar
- 2 cups Greek yogurt
- ½ cup whole milk
- 2 tablespoons maple syrup
- 1¼ teaspoons vanilla bean paste, or 1 whole vanilla bean
- 2 cups heavy cream

CHEFFY NUGGET: For a smoother berry sauce, pour it through a fine-mesh strainer after blending. Push as much through the strainer as possible, pressing with a wooden spoon or spatula, discarding the solids.

dark chocolate bark

WITH CRUNCHY ALMONDS AND SEA SALT

Few desserts are more versatile than chocolate bark; it's a blank canvas you can fill with peppermint candy for the holidays, candy corn for Halloween, or pretzels and potato chips for the Super Bowl. Couverture chocolate is a high-quality type with a high cocoa butter content, making for great shine and the perfect "snap" and ideal for this recipe that gets all broken up. Regular chocolate will work fine, too; it just might melt onto your hands a bit more. Feel free to lick them clean.

1. Line a baking sheet with parchment paper and set aside.

2. In a medium pan, heat the olive oil over medium heat until shimmering. Add the almonds in a single layer and fry, shaking the pan occasionally, until the almonds are deep golden and fragrant. Transfer to a plate lined with paper towels to drain and allow to cool for about 5 minutes, then roughly chop.

3. Roughly chop or break the chocolate into small pieces. Place in the top of a double boiler, or create your own (see Cheffy Nugget). Fill the bottom with 1 to 2 inches of water and bring to a simmer over medium heat. Set the chocolate on top and stir until the chocolate melts.

4. Immediately pour the melted chocolate out onto the prepared baking sheet and smooth into an even layer. Quickly sprinkle the almonds and sea salt on top. Transfer to the fridge to chill until the chocolate is set, at least 1 hour or overnight. Break into pieces and serve.

Leftovers can be stacked in layers with parchment paper in between and stored refrigerated in an airtight container for up to 1 week.

SERVES 4 TO 6

> 2 tablespoons extra-virgin olive oil
> ¼ cup raw almonds
> 12 ounces couverture dark chocolate
> ½ teaspoon flaky sea salt (we like Maldon)

CHEFFY NUGGET: If you don't have a double boiler, don't fret. Bring 1 or 2 inches of water to a boil in a medium pot over medium heat. Place the chocolate in a heatproof bowl that fits over the pot but that doesn't touch the water: The bowl shouldn't be smaller than the pot—it should rest nicely on top, without allowing steam to escape around the sides.

clafoutis with fresh cherries

For the uninitiated, clafoutis is a cross between a giant fluffy pancake and a French crêpe, filled with fresh cherries. Not too sweet, it can be served any time of day. Feel free to swap in different fruits when cherries aren't in season—the batter is too good to be relegated to only one season. Berries, stone fruits, apple, pear—use your imagination!

1. Preheat the oven to 350°F. Melt the butter in a small saucepan over medium heat. Using your fingers, rub it all around an 8-inch ovenproof sauté pan or baking dish.

2. Pit the cherries, if using fresh. In a large bowl, whisk together the milk, cream, eggs, vanilla, vermouth, sugar, and salt until well combined. Add the flour and gently whisk just to incorporate and remove any lumps.

3. Place the buttered skillet or baking dish in the oven to heat, 5 to 10 minutes. Carefully remove from the oven and scatter the cherries evenly over the bottom of the pan. Pour the batter over the cherries and return to the oven. Bake until the clafoutis is just set, 25 to 30 minutes. Allow to cool for at least 10 minutes before serving. Store, covered, in the fridge for up to 2 days.

SERVES 6 TO 8

1 tablespoon unsalted butter
1 cup fresh or thawed frozen cherries
1 cup whole milk
¼ cup heavy cream
2 large eggs
1 teaspoon vanilla extract
2 tablespoons sweet vermouth
¼ cup sugar
¼ teaspoon kosher salt
½ cup all-purpose flour

epic pecan and pumpkin pie

Maybe you can't choose just one pie for Thanksgiving. And maybe you don't feel like making two. Or maybe, like us, you've always been curious to see if you could create an epic fusion pie. Our masterpiece: a layer of pumpkin, topped with a layer of pecan, wrapped up in a homemade crust.

1. In a large bowl, whisk together the flour and salt. Cut the butter and shortening into small pieces and add to the flour. Using your hands, crumble the butter and shortening into the dough to combine until the pieces are no larger than peas. Add the vodka and ice water, 1 tablespoon at a time, until you can gather the dough into a firm ball; it should be moist, but not wet.

2. Pat the dough into a flattened round, then wrap in plastic and refrigerate for at least 1 hour or overnight.

3. Preheat the oven to 425°F.

4. Meanwhile, make the pumpkin filling: In a small bowl, beat the egg. In a large bowl, whisk together the pumpkin, sugar, half the egg (discard the remaining ½ egg), the milk, cream, cinnamon, ginger, cloves, nutmeg, vanilla, and salt.

5. Turn out the chilled dough onto a lightly floured surface and roll it out to a ¼-inch-thick round, slightly larger than the diameter of a 9-inch pie dish. Gently lift the dough onto the pie dish and fit it in, pressing it into the edges and pinching together any tears. Trim off any long overhang from the edges, leaving a small overhang as the dough will shrink back, then press the tines of a fork lightly around the edges for decoration.

6. Add the pumpkin filling to the crust. Place on a baking sheet, transfer to the oven, and bake until just set, about 20 minutes.

7. While the pie bakes, make the pecan filling: In a large bowl, whisk together the eggs and sugar until well combined. Add the corn syrup, melted butter, vanilla, and salt and whisk to combine. Stir in the pecans.

SERVES 8

Crust
- 1½ cups all-purpose flour, plus more for dusting
- ¼ teaspoon kosher salt
- 5 tablespoons cold unsalted butter
- 5 tablespoons shortening, chilled
- 1 tablespoon vodka
- 2 to 3 tablespoons ice water

Pumpkin Filling
- 1 extra-large egg
- ½ cup unsweetened pumpkin puree
- 3 tablespoons sugar
- ¼ cup whole milk
- 2 tablespoons heavy cream
- ½ teaspoon ground cinnamon
- ¼ teaspoon ground ginger
- ⅛ teaspoon ground cloves
- Pinch of ground nutmeg
- ¼ teaspoon vanilla extract
- Pinch of kosher salt

Pecan Filling
- 2 extra-large eggs
- ⅓ cup sugar
- ½ cup dark corn syrup
- 1½ tablespoons unsalted butter, melted
- ½ teaspoon vanilla extract
- ⅛ teaspoon kosher salt
- ¾ cup chopped pecans

8. After the pie has baked for 20 minutes, remove from the oven and gently pour in the pecan filling. Return to the oven and bake until the pecan filling is almost set, about 30 minutes. Reduce the oven temperature to 350°F and continue baking until the crust is golden and the filling is no longer wiggly, about 15 minutes longer.

9. Remove the pie from the oven and allow to cool for at least 10 minutes before serving. (If you're not eating it right away, cover it with plastic wrap and store in the fridge for up to 3 days.)

CHEFFY NUGGET: If you notice your crust beginning to brown too quickly in the middle of cooking, lightly cover the crust with foil, being careful not to cover the filling.

mini chocolate chip cookie
ice cream bowls

These cookie bowls were invented on a quiet Friday in the Plated Test Kitchen—because why wouldn't we use a slow day to invent a new edible vessel for ice cream? We tested a few cookie dough recipes, but ultimately found the ideal, perfectly chewy ones that are just the right texture for molding into muffin tins. With a touch of ice cream, pretty much every bite is the perfect bite.

1. Preheat the oven to 350°F.

2. Generously grease 12 cups of a muffin tin with some softened butter and set aside. Cut out small squares of foil to fit inside the muffin cups (1 per cup), and set aside for later.

3. Melt the butter in a microwave or in a small saucepan over medium heat.

4. In a medium bowl, sift together the flour, baking soda, and salt.

5. In a separate medium bowl, using an electric mixer, cream together the melted butter, brown sugar, and granulated sugar. Beat the vanilla, whole egg, and egg yolk into the butter-sugar mixture until light and creamy. Stir the flour mixture into the wet ingredients until just blended, taking care not to overmix. Stir in the chocolate chips. Cover the dough with plastic wrap and chill in the fridge for at least 30 minutes or overnight (or freeze for 20 minutes).

6. Scoop out about 1½ tablespoons dough and roll into a ball. Flatten slightly into a disc and press into the bottom of a muffin cup, pressing down and nudging to fit into the space without going up the sides—this is the "bottom" of the cookie bowl. (If the dough becomes too warm or soft, rechill for 5 minutes before continuing.) Repeat 12 times.

7. Scoop out larger balls of dough and rolls into logs with your hands. Flatten slightly, then wrap around the insides of the muffin cups. This isn't an exact science, so add or subtract dough as needed. Press the dough into the cups, shaping to adhere and get the dough even with the top of

SERVES 6 TO 8

12 tablespoons (1½ sticks) unsalted butter, plus softened butter for the muffin tin
2 cups all-purpose flour
½ teaspoon baking soda
½ teaspoon kosher salt
1 cup packed light brown sugar
½ cup granulated sugar
1 tablespoon vanilla extract
1 large egg
1 large egg yolk
1½ cups semisweet mini chocolate chips
Your favorite ice cream, for serving (we like vanilla)

(recipe continues)

the muffin cup. Be sure to try to flatten the dough against the sides and avoiding sloping into the middle too much. The bottoms and sides should touch to create one cohesive "bowl."

8. Carefully fit the foil square into the center of each cookie bowl and weight down (pie weights or a few dried beans work well), being sure your weights are contained within the foil and not pressing into your dough. Bake the cookie bowls until they begin to brown around the edges, 18 to 20 minutes.

9. Gently remove the foil and beans and allow the cookie bowls to cool for about 10 minutes. Invert the muffin tin and tap the bottoms to loosen the bowls. Fill with your favorite ice cream and serve immediately.

jam and citrus parfaits

WITH WHIPPED CREAM

A no-bake confection, parfaits are ideal for a last-minute dessert or as a simple finish to an elaborately prepared meal. Mix and match with ladyfingers, angel food cake, or sponge cake, and swap in different flavors of jam for variety. We love serving these in clear glass vessels to show off their colorful layers.

1. In a medium bowl, whisk together the cream and powdered sugar until stiff peaks form, about 3 minutes. Place in the fridge to chill for about 10 minutes.

2. Meanwhile, halve the oranges and squeeze the juice into a separate medium bowl. Add the strawberry jam. Break the pound cake into bite-size pieces.

3. Divide one-third of the pound cake, breaking it up if necessary, among parfait glasses, short, wide glasses, or bowls. Top with one-third of the jam mixture, followed by one-third of the whipped cream. Repeat the layers with the remaining pound cake, jam, and whipped cream. Serve immediately or chill in the fridge for up to 1 hour.

SERVES 4 TO 6

> 1 cup heavy cream
> ¼ cup powdered sugar
> 3 oranges
> ¾ cup strawberry jam
> 1 8-inch pound cake

CHEFFY NUGGET: Keep your heavy cream in the fridge until right before using; it will whip best when it's chilled.

key lime pie

WITH WHIPPED CREAM

Shockingly simple, the filling for these tart and gooey Key lime pies only needs three ingredients. Sandwiched between a crunchy graham cracker crust and a dollop of whipped cream, it's summer dessert heaven. Tiny, seasonal Key limes are a labor of love to juice—if you're not up to the task, bottled juice works just fine, or even lemons as a backup.

1. Preheat the oven to 350°F.

2. In a food processor, pulse the graham crackers into fine crumbs. Melt the butter over medium heat and add to the food processor along with the granulated sugar and a pinch of salt. Pulse until fully incorporated. Press the mixture into the bottom of a 9-inch pie dish. Bake until the crust is golden, about 12 minutes. Leave the oven on, but reduce the temperature to 325°F.

3. While the crust bakes, zest 3 of the Key limes. In a large bowl, whisk the eggs. Add the condensed milk and whisk to combine. While whisking, slowly whisk in the Key lime juice.

4. Pour the filling into the baked crust and return to the oven. Bake until the filling has puffed slightly, about 30 minutes. Remove from the oven and allow to cool completely.

5. While the pie cools, in a medium bowl, using an electric mixer or a whisk, beat the cream and powdered sugar until stiff peaks form. Refrigerate until ready to serve.

6. Garnish the pie with the Key lime zest and whipped cream before slicing.

SERVES 8

12 full graham cracker sheets
5 tablespoons unsalted butter
¼ cup granulated sugar
½ cup Key lime juice, store-bought or fresh (from about 50 Key limes)
3 large eggs
1 14-ounce can condensed milk
½ cup heavy cream
2 tablespoons powdered sugar
Kosher salt

glossary

Cooking lingo might be "all Greek" to some of you, so here's what we mean when we say . . .

Bake: Cook in the oven at a medium temperature, usually below 400°F. Commonly refers to doughs and pastries.

Boil: Cook a liquid over high heat, looking for large, rolling bubbles in the center of the pot.

Braise: Cook over low heat, partly submerged in liquid, for an extended period of time.

Broil: Cook just below the heat source, for a short period of time.

Brown: Cook in a pan until literally browned and a crust is beginning to form.

Caramelize: Cook until tender and just beginning to brown. This technique is used to brown the sugars in ingredients, whether naturally occurring or added.

Cure: Smother an ingredient in a salt-and-sugar mixture to pull out its moisture and change its texture. This technique works for preserving a protein, and is also a method to concentrate flavor.

Deglaze: Add liquid to a pan with browned bits on the bottom to loosen them, by scraping them up with a wooden spoon. This technique helps pick up these flavorful bits, called *fond*, which can be the beginning of a sauce or braising liquid.

Dice: Cut an ingredient into cubes. Imagine actual game dice, like for Monopoly, and use that as a size gauge for medium dice. Small dice are, well, smaller, and large dice are about 1 inch.

Drain: Discard the liquid, like pasta water, reserving only the solids.

Dredge: Dip into flour, bread crumbs, batter, cornmeal, or other fine-textured or liquid mixtures to coat completely.

Emulsify: To combine fat and acid (oil and vinegar for example) to create a thick, unctuous texture. Whisking in a figure-eight motion will help best achieve this.

Fold: Gently incorporate one ingredient into another by simultaneously swiping the spatula around the bowl, while rotating the bowl, and then through the middle. This technique is often used for desserts, typically for batters, whipped cream, or whipped egg whites.

Marinate: Allow an ingredient to sit in a liquid or dry rub mixture to impart flavor before cooking.

Mince: Cut up an ingredient as finely as possible. Think dicing, but even smaller.

PRODUCE TECHNIQUES

Artichokes: To prepare an artichoke (assuming you're not eating it whole, as in Date Night (page 154), slice off the top third of the artichoke, then peel off two or three layers of tough outer leaves. Peel the stems, then halve or quarter the artichokes lengthwise. Scoop out the furry choke, then roast or pan-fry.

Asparagus: The bottom quarter of the stalk is quite woody, and should be removed and discarded before using. Simply bend the asparagus near the woody end and it will snap off naturally.

Butternut Squash: We recommend that you save yourself some time and buy butternut squash already peeled and cut up. Since you rarely cook butternut squash whole or halved, this prep shortcut is super useful. If you *do* want to tackle the whole squash, peel it, then halve crosswise. Scoop out and discard the seeds, then cut as directed in your recipe.

Celery Root: Trim the gnarled parts off the top and bottom using a sharp knife and sit flat. Cut around the tough skin to remove it. The flesh is much softer and easier to cut as directed.

Fava Beans: Fresh fava beans require a bit of work to peel, but this spring delicacy is well worth the effort. Open the pods at the seams and remove the beans. Blanch the beans briefly in boiling water, then peel off the tough light-green skins to reveal the darker green beans underneath.

Fennel: To use the fennel bulb, begin by trimming off the long stalks. Cut the bulb in half through the root, then use the tip of your knife to cut out the tough core from each half. Prepare as directed.

Fiddlehead Ferns: These curly, mythical-looking vegetables can be really dirty. Trim the tails, then soak them in a bowl of cold water, shaking gently to remove dirt. Scoop them out of the dirty water: Don't drain them into a colander, as this will put you back at square one. Blanch in boiling water to soften before cooking as directed.

Leeks: Because of their many layers, leeks can hide a lot of dirt. Cut them up as your recipe indicates, then soak the pieces in a large bowl of water, gently shaking to allow the dirt to sink to the bottom. Scoop them out of the dirty water: Don't drain them into a colander, as this will put you back at square one.

Rutabaga: A rutabaga can sometimes be the size of a bowling ball, so buying it pre-cubed is ideal. If you have a whole one on your hands, peel it, then slice off chunks and cut them as directed.

APPENDIX B
glossary

Cooking lingo might be "all Greek" to some of you, so here's what we mean when we say . . .

Bake: Cook in the oven at a medium temperature, usually below 400°F. Commonly refers to doughs and pastries.

Boil: Cook a liquid over high heat, looking for large, rolling bubbles in the center of the pot.

Braise: Cook over low heat, partly submerged in liquid, for an extended period of time.

Broil: Cook just below the heat source, for a short period of time.

Brown: Cook in a pan until literally browned and a crust is beginning to form.

Caramelize: Cook until tender and just beginning to brown. This technique is used to brown the sugars in ingredients, whether naturally occurring or added.

Cure: Smother an ingredient in a salt-and-sugar mixture to pull out its moisture and change its texture. This technique works for preserving a protein, and is also a method to concentrate flavor.

Deglaze: Add liquid to a pan with browned bits on the bottom to loosen them, by scraping them up with a wooden spoon. This technique helps pick up these flavorful bits, called *fond*, which can be the beginning of a sauce or braising liquid.

Dice: Cut an ingredient into cubes. Imagine actual game dice, like for Monopoly, and use that as a size gauge for medium dice. Small dice are, well, smaller, and large dice are about 1 inch.

Drain: Discard the liquid, like pasta water, reserving only the solids.

Dredge: Dip into flour, bread crumbs, batter, cornmeal, or other fine-textured or liquid mixtures to coat completely.

Emulsify: To combine fat and acid (oil and vinegar for example) to create a thick, unctuous texture. Whisking in a figure-eight motion will help best achieve this.

Fold: Gently incorporate one ingredient into another by simultaneously swiping the spatula around the bowl, while rotating the bowl, and then through the middle. This technique is often used for desserts, typically for batters, whipped cream, or whipped egg whites.

Marinate: Allow an ingredient to sit in a liquid or dry rub mixture to impart flavor before cooking.

Mince: Cut up an ingredient as finely as possible. Think dicing, but even smaller.

key lime pie

WITH WHIPPED CREAM

Shockingly simple, the filling for these tart and gooey Key lime pies only needs three ingredients. Sandwiched between a crunchy graham cracker crust and a dollop of whipped cream, it's summer dessert heaven. Tiny, seasonal Key limes are a labor of love to juice—if you're not up to the task, bottled juice works just fine, or even lemons as a backup.

1. Preheat the oven to 350°F.

2. In a food processor, pulse the graham crackers into fine crumbs. Melt the butter over medium heat and add to the food processor along with the granulated sugar and a pinch of salt. Pulse until fully incorporated. Press the mixture into the bottom of a 9-inch pie dish. Bake until the crust is golden, about 12 minutes. Leave the oven on, but reduce the temperature to 325°F.

3. While the crust bakes, zest 3 of the Key limes. In a large bowl, whisk the eggs. Add the condensed milk and whisk to combine. While whisking, slowly whisk in the Key lime juice.

4. Pour the filling into the baked crust and return to the oven. Bake until the filling has puffed slightly, about 30 minutes. Remove from the oven and allow to cool completely.

5. While the pie cools, in a medium bowl, using an electric mixer or a whisk, beat the cream and powdered sugar until stiff peaks form. Refrigerate until ready to serve.

6. Garnish the pie with the Key lime zest and whipped cream before slicing.

SERVES 8

- 12 **full graham cracker sheets**
- 5 **tablespoons unsalted butter**
- ¼ **cup granulated sugar**
- ½ **cup Key lime juice, store-bought or fresh (from about 50 Key limes)**
- 3 **large eggs**
- 1 **14-ounce can condensed milk**
- ½ **cup heavy cream**
- 2 **tablespoons powdered sugar**
- **Kosher salt**

seasonal produce guide

Sometimes when we're working four months ahead on recipes in the Plated Test Kitchen, in the dead of winter, we find ourselves in dire need of a reminder of what's in season when. So we put one together! This outline is what we use to plan seasonal recipes all y`ear round. We've also included some tips and tricks for preparation. Here's to enjoying what's fresh in every meal you make!

FALL AND WINTER

ROOTS	GOURDS	FRUITS	GREENS	EVERYTHING IN BETWEEN
parsnips	butternut squash	apples	kale	snow peas
celery root	delicata squash (fall only)	pears	Swiss chard	radicchio
turnips	acorn squash	figs (early fall)	escarole	Brussels sprouts
rutabaga	spaghetti squash	grapefruit	mustard greens	cauliflower
sweet potatoes	dumpling squash	oranges	cabbage	
potatoes	kabocha squash	blood oranges		
sunchokes	blue Hubbard squash	clementines		
jicama	pumpkin	tangerines		
		pomegranates		
		Concord grapes (early fall)		
		quince		

SPRING AND SUMMER

YEAR ROUND

FRUITS	GREENS	VEGETABLES		
tomatoes	arugula	eggplant	ramps (early spring)	beets
cherries	butter lettuce	bell peppers	fiddlehead ferns	carrots
peaches	little gem (spring)	sweet peas (spring)	radishes	broccoli
grapes	mâche	sugar snap peas (spring)	garlic scapes (spring)	mushrooms
watermelon	watercress	fava beans (spring)	scallions	
strawberries	spinach	zucchini	corn	
blueberries	basil (summer)	summer squash	green beans	
raspberries		cucumbers	morels (spring)	
cantaloupe		asparagus		
honeydew melon		artichokes		
rhubarb		leeks		
apricots				

acknowledgments

It goes without saying that this book would not have come into being without Plated. To all the dedicated, inspiring people we have the privilege of working with day in and day out, and to all our customers: Thank you for making us realize it is possible to do what you love every single day. Nick and Josh, thank you for entrusting precious recipes to us week after week; we forgive you for overstepping your taste-testing bounds.

A giant thank-you to our unbelievably talented photographer, Robert Bredvad, who makes us look good on a daily basis by transforming our food into food porn. And to Maeve Sheridan, our prop stylist, who stuck with us through two apartments, three offices, and varying amounts of limited space to cram props. You've managed to turn any plate and setting into a true work of art, while also keeping us fueled with doughnuts and fancy coffee. You both make the magic happen.

Thank you to Suzanne Lenzer and her assistants, Kate Schmidt and Erica Clark. Through your food-styling talents, you were able to take our vision and bring it to life on the plate (and page). We got a crash course in styling watching you work, and we're so grateful you were a part of this book.

To Michelle Kresch . . . where to begin. Thank you for putting up with our kitchen antics, making us the world's best cupcakes when our blood sugar (and spirits) were low, and keeping us young and cool. We really could not have finished this book without you.

To Tina Mohanty, thank you for adding "publishing lawyer" to your résumé for us.

Thank you to Amanda Englander, our editor, for taking a chance on us and holding our hands through our first book (and several meltdowns). You sweat the small stuff in the best way, and our work is all the better for it. To our copy editor, Kate Slate, thank you for your meticulous work on our book, and for making it shiny and polished.

Reduce: Simmer a liquid until it decreases in volume (and increases in flavor).

Render: Slowly melt out the fat, creating crispy bacon or poultry skin.

Rest: Remove your just-finished protein from the pan and allow it to sit, undisturbed, for 5 to 15 minutes before cutting into it.

Roast: Cook in the oven at a high temperature, usually 400°F or higher. Refers mostly to proteins and vegetables.

Sauté: Cook quickly in a little bit of fat, often just to soften.

Score: Cut a crosshatch pattern in food without going all the way through. Common for ingredients like duck skin or dough.

Sear: Cook quickly over very high heat to brown the outside of an ingredient, typically proteins.

Simmer: Cook something just below the boiling point, looking for small bubbles around the edges of the pot.

Strain: Discard the solids from a liquid, like aromatics from a broth, reserving the liquid.

Whipping to stiff peaks: Whip or beat egg whites or cream until stiff, pointed caps form and stay when you lift the whisk.

Zest: Peel off the very outer colored layer of a citrus, leaving behind the white pith, using a zester, a vegetable peeler, or even a fine grater.

To everyone else at Clarkson Potter, we can't believe we're included in your roster of authors. Going to our first meeting in your offices for our pitch was the most nerve-racking and exciting experience of our lives, and we couldn't be more honored to have you publish our book.

Elana would also like to thank her friends and family for being the most enthusiastic taste testers, restaurant critics, and recipe guinea pigs. Specifically her sous chefs Mom, Dad, Josh, Bup, Gary, Steve, and Tammy.

Suzanne would also like to thank her parents for instilling and encouraging an obsession with food and cooking from an early age (for better or worse), and Deb for being a coconspirator in at least the eating part. To her friends, thanks for always supplying the chef with wine. To Paul, she promises to cook at least half these meals for you over your lifetimes. She loves you all.

To the Plated customers, it has been a pleasure to cook with you and have a seat at your table. Thank you for making our food and sharing your photos and stories with us. Nothing turns a bad day around like browsing through your #platedpics. There would be no book without you.

index

about the authors

Elana Karp joined Plated in 2012, in the earliest of days. She is a graduate of Cornell University and Le Cordon Bleu in Paris, where she learned the value of French butter and perfect technique. Before turning her attention to food, Elana taught second graders in Harlem for Teach for America. She then worked for Sur La Table and started her own catering and after-school culinary education program for children, which fueled her passion for teaching people how easy and fun cooking can be. Nothing makes Elana happier than bringing people together into the kitchen over food. Her last meal on earth would be an overstuffed grilled cheese with lots of ketchup. Or maybe a roast chicken with creamy mashed potatoes. It's too hard to pick just one!

Suzanne Lehrer Dumaine joined Plated in 2013. She is a graduate of Dartmouth College and the International Culinary Center in New York, which she attended after the poignant realization that cooking food could actually become a job. Having worked as a recipe developer and a recipe editor at Food Network, Suzanne loves showing home cooks that with the right instruction and a clearly written recipe, they can pull off way more in their kitchens than they ever expected. Her work has been published in *Time Out New York,* Serious Eats, The Daily Meal, and VanityFair.com. Her last meal on earth would be a giant stack of pizzas, alternating Neopolitan and New York–style.

Together, Elana and Suzanne have written over 1,500 recipes for Plated.